MIRROR FEATURES PRESENTS

Mr. Crabtree Goes Fishing

by

Bernard Venables

50th Anniversary Edition

Published by
MAP MARKETING LIMITED, OMEGA HOUSE, SMUGGLERS WAY, LONDON SW18 1AZ ISBN 978-1-84252-131-1

The Fisherman in winter

TO many fishermen the end of the season comes about 30th September. In a fine year, it might perhaps, be prolonged until the end of October. In any case they think of it as an occupation for the leafy months. It is associated in their minds with the hum of bees and the drowsiness of warm days.

This is certainly a very lovely part of the fisherman's year, but it is very far from being all of it if he is to get from it all that there is to be had. The winter can give him such an extension of his pleasure as he has no conception of until he has tried it.

I think that for most anglers an appreciation of landscape and a delight in the sounds of nature are bound up with their pleasure in angling; and for a great many this means leafy banks, the scent of hay, birdsong and the charm of seeing animals about their business. And all this, they feel, is something that passes with the summer. In winter, they think of everything as being held in a deep cold sleep.

This is far from being true, as any winter fisherman can tell you. In winter the otter may still be seen by the lucky fisherman. The heron still stalks about the shallows in search of little fish. The kingfisher and the dipper have not departed, and in fact the dipper sings more sweetly from December on than it does at any

other time. Many others of the waterside animals are still abroad, even the squirrel that so many believe sleeps the winter through. It can be seen in all but the hardest weather. There is no dead stop to nature as the town dweller seems to suppose. When the very last of the bloom and leaf has left the banks, it is only quite a short pause before catkins and the earliest blossoms bestrew it again.

And in that pause there is no real stop. A fox has jumped from beneath my very feet in the dried sedges on an iron hard day in December. The weather has as lovely a procession of change as it has at any other time. Mild, pale blue skies give way to inky threatening ones, and those in turn to the crack and glitter of sharp frost. Any weather but a steady downpour is a pleasure on the river bank. The leaves may have gone from the trees, but they are none the less beautiful for that. However familiar your river bank, if you know it only in summer its winter loveliness will be a revelation to you. Then your eye can dwell on the clean and massive strength of oak and ash and beech, and see the pale clear colours of them. You can find pleasure in the brilliant crimson of the osier, and in the elegant lean and droop of the willows over the water.

But of course you do not come to the water merely to find a gentle pleasure in landscape and birds and trees. Nor need you do so. You have come to fish and you can do this to very good purpose. Some of your fishes of summer will no longer be feeding and therefore ready to be angled for, but of the others some will show you better sport now than ever they did in summer. And of those properly regarded as summer fish, there are days throughout the winter that will bring them from their torpor unless it be a very hard season.

The tench and the carp are most justly regarded as fish of summer, but there are many of them that have found their way to the fisherman's keep-net on a mild day in winter. In the south particularly, the middle hours of a warm day will bring them all on feed. Of bream too this is true. On these days, large catches have been made in the heart of winter. As for the barbel, in recent years they have flouted every rule that is said to govern them, by feeding lustily almost throughout the winter. These winters, it is true, have been mild, but it is something that it has been well worth while to set out specifically to catch barbel at the end of December.

But though all these fishes may provide occasional sport to vary the fisherman's days, it is not on them that he relies. In most places they are no more than windfalls and it is not for them that a man becomes a convinced winter fisherman. It is for those fish that in the winter reach their full prime, and only then give the angler the whole sport of which they are capable.

The roach, I suppose, is the most popular fish of all. It is a good fish to fish for in the summer. Its subtlety, the difficulty of its deception, ensure that. But it must be admitted that as a fighter it does not rank very high. In winter, however, it is another fish. Its shy cunning is not in the least blunted, and it develops as well a muscular power unknown in the summer fish. A roach then, of a pound and a half, will show its mettle.

The rudd of winter is equally improved. In fact its showing at the end of a line will be even better than that of the roach. For this is a deeper fish, a more solid and weighty fish. A day with rudd in the closing months of the season can be a red-letter day.

As for the chub, between that of summer and that of winter there is just no comparison. Let us admit that the chub of summer is too often a lank and spiritless thing that gives way with scarcely a struggle. But how different it is in winter. Then a chub of over three pounds will give you all the fight you can want. I have seen many on the Wye, that, seeming irresistible, have plunged to freedom in the roots.

But of all the fishes of winter, there is none perhaps, that so comes into its own as the pike. The limp and flaccid fish of summer becomes a fierce and powerful fighter that inspires thousands of fishermen to its pursuit, whatever the weather.

Now let's join Mr. Crabtree and Peter, and see what winter sport we can have in their company.

The Crabtrees start their fishing year on a river that is almost flooded.

SO the Crabtrees have decided to start their fishing year in January. They could not do better. For as we have discussed on the previous page, this is a time of the year when many fish have come to their best. Their last spawning season is long behind them, and they have been fully recovered from it for several months now. They are in fact, building up to their maximum strength for the next one which will come to them in the spring.

But will Mr. Crabtree and Peter find the same river as they saw in the summer, or will it present them with different problems? As you will see, the river is very different indeed from its summer self. Winter fishing often does provide conditions which at first sight seem much more difficult to cope with than those of summer.

Here they find a swirling waste of water that does not suggest that it could hold life at all. What, they might think, could live in that rushing river, brimful, heavy with the soil it has disturbed from its banks? It is impossible to see an inch into it.

But, they must remind themselves, the fish are still there. They cannot leave the river. They must have tucked themselves in somewhere. And if the fish can be found, they may be feeding.

WE'LL HAVE TO FISH RIGHT ON THE BOTTOM— WE'D BETTER USE LEDGER TACKLE

HERE'S THE LEDGER— A PIERCED BULLET THREADED ON THE CAST, WITH A SPLIT SHOT PINCHED ON AT THE BOTTOM TO STOP THE BULLET GOING LOWER, AND A Nº 10 HOOK—TO-GUT BELOW THAT

NOW WE'VE TIED THE LEDGER TO THE LINE, WE'LL PUT ON THE BAIT—THE TAIL OF A LOB WORM— THAT'S THE ORDINARY BIG GARDEN WORM YOU KNOW

33

NOW WE CAST OUT THE TACKLE INTO THE EDDY—

THEN WE PUT THE ROD IN THIS REST MADE WITH A FORKED STICK, AND REEL UP THE LINE SO THAT IT IS TAUT FROM ROD TOP TO BAIT

THE RIVER IS VERY HIGH AND COLOURED SO THE CRABTREES ARE LEDGERING IN A DEEP HOLE OUT OF THE WAY OF THE CURRENT

NOW THAT WE'VE CAST OUT, PETER, WE PROP THE ROD IN A CLEFT STICK AND PUT ON THE CHECK OF THE REEL

34

AND WE REEL UP THE LINE SO THAT IT'S TAUT BETWEEN ROD TOP AND BAIT

NOW AWAIT EVENTS AND WATCH THE ROD TOP

WE'LL THROW IN SOME FRAGMENTS OF WORM TO INTEREST THEM IN OUR BAIT

Where does common-sense suggest the fish would go under these circumstances? Surely anywhere where they could escape the force of the current. Into the holes under the tree roots, into the eddies that lie behind shoulders of bank, into cattle-drink bays in the bank. These are the places that Mr. Crabtree looks for. He finds a cattle drink, a place where in summer the cattle would go down the bank to stand in shallow water. Now it is deep and a fine harbourage for fish that must escape the force of the current.

But it is more than a mere refuge. That violent current is bringing down more than just mere soil and debris to be a nuisance to fish and fisherman. It is also bringing down many things on which fish can feed. It is also providing a chance for heavy feeding at a season when many forms of life on which fish feed are dormant. Most fish will eat worms when they are to be had, and this flood is washing down great quantities of them. It is also washing out from the banks all sorts of grubs that have gone there to hibernate. It will also bring many other small forms of life,

THE CRABTREES' LEDGER TACKLE IS IN THE DEEP HOLE

YOU SEE, PETER, ALL THE FISH ARE COLLECTED IN THIS HOLE AND THEY'RE NOSING ABOUT TO FIND FOOD ON THE BOTTOM

AND WHEN THEY FIND THE BITS OF WORM THEY'LL BE ON THE LOOK-OUT FOR MORE —INCLUDING OUR BAIT

35

THERE GOES THE ROD TOP! SOMETHING'S AT THE BAIT

NOW STRIKE— AND IT'S ON!

DON'T KNOW YET WHAT IT IS. ANYTHING CAN TURN UP IN THIS HOLE

THE CRABTREES HAVE HOOKED A FISH IN THE HOLE

GET THE NET UNDER IT, PETER—IT'S A ROACH— AND A GOOD ONE

THERE IT IS, A ROACH OF ABOUT 1½ lb — A NICE FISH!

POP IT IN THE KEEP-NET, PETER

OUT WITH THE TACKLE AGAIN AND SEE WHAT ELSE WE CAN GET

IT MAY BE ANOTHER ROACH, OR—

36

but Mr. Crabtree knows that certainly worms and gentles will not appear novelties to the fish. They could take either of those with the confidence that it was their natural food. And of those, experience has shown Mr. Crabtree that worms are the better. For heavy coloured water there is no bait to beat a worm.

There are various kinds of worm, the red worm, the marsh worm, the brandling, and the lobworm, and of these just the tail of the lobworm has proved to be a bait that most fish will take under these conditions. It is small enough to be taken by a roach and big enough to interest a chub.

Where should this bait be fished? Should it be suspended on float-tackle to circulate round the eddy that has formed in the cattle-drink? It is highly unlikely that the fish would find it then, for they could not see it. Usually under these conditions the fish will be on the bottom, and it is there that the bait must be. The fish will be grubbing about on the bottom expecting to find food there. They still could not see the bait, not at least until they

were right on top of it. But their sense of smell will help to guide them to it.

Ledger tackle is very suitable for this fishing. No plumbing of the depth is necessary, which saves disturbing the swim, and it can be made to lie on the bottom in a natural way. It is also a sensitive method which catches the gently biting roach as readily as the bold biting chub.

As will be seen from the pictures, the population of an eddy or hole such as this can be a very mixed one. That gives a special excitement to the fishing. It is fishing that calls for no great skill but it is fascinating none the less. Anything may be beneath that murk of water. The fisherman never knows from moment to moment what he may be fighting next. It may be a roach of

a few ounces or it may be a chub of five pounds. If the weather has turned mild it may even be a great carp or a barbel if there are such in the river being fished. It is an extreme case of the thing that is one of the greatest fascinations to the fisherman, one of the basic things that make him go fishing - the mystery of another element, the casting of a line into the unknown. And for the really keen fisherman who must go fishing whatever the conditions, it is some sort of fishing, which is better than sitting at home longing for the river.

For Peter it is a fairly certain success when his skill might not be sufficient to get him any under other conditions. Once the novice fisherman has tasted success, his enthusiasm will be kindled and he will persevere to gain the skill necessary for other fishing.

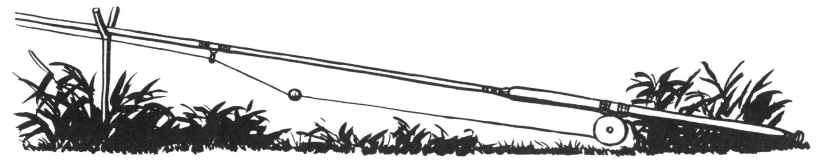

Though, as we have seen, the rod top will show when a fish has taken the bait on ledger tackle, there is a more sensitive indicator. Squeeze a small ball of ground-bait round the line between the reel and the butt ring. Watch this ball, it will give instant notice when a fish takes the bait.

Something about Mr. Crabtree's tackle . . .

RODS

In the beginning the new angler will fish with one rod. He will use this for all his bottom fishing and manage quite well with it. Indeed the delight of his first reasonably good rod will be so great that for a time he will want nothing else. But after a time he will become aware that different rods for different fish and types of fishing are a help.

Split cane.   Whole cane.

Here is the rod that Mr. Crabtree uses for roach fishing on many waters of the slower kind and on still water when he is fishing for roach. But it would also make an excellent all-round rod for the beginner. It is sharp in action, the slightest movement of the wrist causing an instant strike. Though it can be used for most fish, it is most suitable for quick biters such as roach and dace.

Split cane.   Whole cane.

This is a stronger rod and not so sharp in its action. Mr. Crabtree uses it for carp, bream, tench, chub, and barbel. On fast heavy rivers like the Hampshire Avon he uses it for roach too. On rivers of that type it is necessary to cast heavy float tackle long distances, and this is the rod for that. Striking to a roach bite thirty yards away does not require the same sharp strike as when it is under the rod top.

REELS

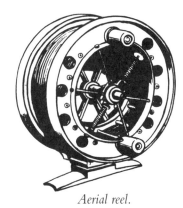
Aerial reel.

Flick'em type reel.

Old fashioned star-back reel.

There are many reels for the bottom fisherman to choose from, and the beginner will be less fussy than he will be later on. As a learner he can do quite well with a cheap reel. He may be lucky enough to come across a good old star-back such as Mr. Crabtree has. These are of wood, metal lined, and some of them are very good indeed. But the time is certain to come when he will want one of the beautiful reels for the float fisherman that are produced today. Of these none is better than the Aerial, a lovely reel which is equally good for spinning or float fishing. Also very good is the Flick'em type. Both are very free-running.

FLOATS

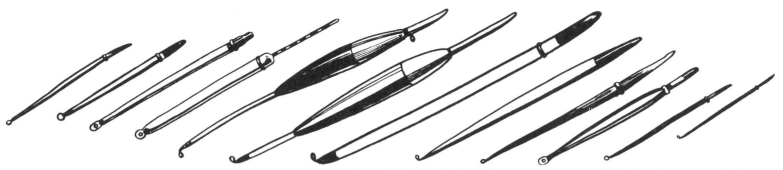

Floats are fascinating little things and there is no end to the variety of them. With some anglers collecting them becomes a hobby. But it must never be forgotten what is their purpose. That is to support the tackle in the water and show when a fish bites. Different waters and different fish call for very different floats. Fishing in still water for roach needs something to carry only one or at most two shot, and which is as inconspicuous as possible. The tiniest quill is right. But for heavy fast water a pelican quill or a cork-bodied float is necessary.

HOOKS

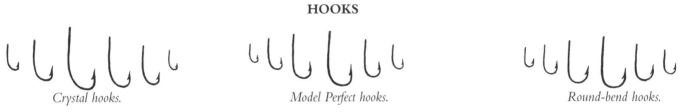

Crystal hooks.   *Model Perfect hooks.*   *Round-bend hooks.*

The fisherman fishes with many different baits, and he needs different hooks to suit them. Model Perfect hooks are very good, and the nearest approach to an all-round hook. But to get the best results a special hook should be used for worm baits, the round bend hook. For most other baits either the crystal or the Model Perfect can be used. Some anglers swear by gilt hooks.

LEADS

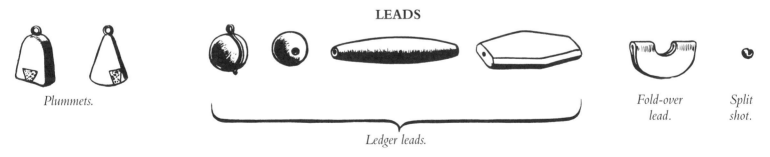

Plummets.   *Ledger leads.*   *Fold-over lead.*   *Split shot.*

The fisherman uses leads of many kinds and here are some of those that Mr. Crabtree uses. A plummet is essential to the float fisherman. The proper use of it can make all the difference between a blank and a good day. We have already seen something of ledgering and there is a wide choice of leads for this. The heavier the current the larger the lead. Coffin leads are good in heavy water. Split shot are always being used. They can be had in various sizes. Half-moon leads are very useful. In small sizes they can replace split shot, in larger sizes they are useful for spinning.

9

The river in winter

Explanation of symbols –
R – roach
P – perch
PK – pike
C – chub
D – dace

In studying this illustration of the river in winter, the first thing to be noticed is that all fish tend to avoid the full force of the main current. On many rivers of average flow, these main currents would in summer carry a population of such fish as roach and dace, and in the earlier part of the season at least, chub as well. But in winter the river will have gained force. Roach and dace will still be found in the current, but in the easier parts of it. Many of them will also be found in the eddies. The chub will have become almost entirely a fish of the deep eddies, though it will still be possible to find them where the current runs softly under the trees. The perch too will have left the current, and will have sought the deep holes. The one shown here against the camp-shedding is particularly to their liking. The pike will now certainly be lying in the quiet water. He likes a covered place where he can get his tail under the roots of a tree or in the sedges that grow down into the water. Any quiet place protected from the current may be expected to hold fish.

11

The Crabtrees are going to the best coarse fishing river in England.

THERE is no river in England which is more exciting to the imagination of the coarse fisherman than the Hampshire Avon. No other river so teems with monstrous fish of various species. Its pike grow to great size, as was shown in 1944 when a new British record for this species was set up by a fish taken at Fordingbridge which weighed $37\frac{1}{2}$ lb. Its chub are plentiful and enormous. In the 1948-49 Daily Mirror Club Angling Competition the Christchurch Angling Club entered a long list of chub between 5 lb. 4 oz. and 5 lb. 14 oz., and from time to time fish of between six and seven pounds are taken. If the British record for chub is to be beaten it is more than likely that it will be the Avon that does it.

Its roach are scarcely less impressive, though it has a formidable rival here in the Norfolk Broads district. The same entry of the Christchurch Club included two fish of 3 lb. 1 oz. and 3 lb., as well as many between two and three pounds. And then its barbel! Though the barbel was not originally native to the river, since it was introduced it has thrived amazingly, and most seasons fish are caught over ten pounds, some running up to over fourteen pounds.

For the angler who wishes to furnish glass cases, the Avon is the inevitable Mecca. There is nowhere else he can go knowing that if he perseveres and fishes well, he will sooner or later catch great fish.

But it is no novice's playground. Coarse bungling will never bring results. The angler must know his business and he must teach himself to know this river. If he comes from other parts of the country where local conditions are quite different, and makes no modifications of his methods to suit the Avon, he will not get good results. Midland anglers accustomed to gentle currents or still water that dictate ultra-fine tackle will get nowhere if they do not adapt themselves very considerably. Crow quill floats and six or eight x gut with one or two shot would be swept away before the fish had a chance to see the bait. The stiff, lightning striking rods of many roach fishers are out of place too. Much of the time the strike is so far from the fisherman that even if it started as a lightning strike, it would not reach the fish as such.

The first consideration is to get the bait down to the fish, for the Avon is a strong river, a deep heavy river that calls for tackle that elsewhere might be considered coarse. The thing to do is to strike a happy medium in the weight of tackle. Mr. Crabtree gives an idea of what is practical.

But the heavy water of the Avon is not the only way in which this river differs from many others. For it is a chalk stream,

FOR THE F.K. WALLIS CAST I START WITH MY HANDS LIKE THIS – THE LINE CAUGHT OVER MY LEFT THUMB, AND MY RIGHT HAND HOLDING THE ROD

THE LITTLE FINGER OF MY RIGHT HAND IS ON THE EDGE OF THE REEL READY TO FLICK IT

I SWING THE ROD ROUND TO MY LEFT, KEEPING THE LINE TAUT OVER MY THUMB – THEN SWING FORWARD

THEN AS THE LINE FLIES FORWARD I FLICK THE REEL INTO ACTION WITH MY LITTLE FINGER

I KEEP MY LITTLE FINGER ON THE DRUM WITH SENSITIVE PRESSURE TO STOP THE REEL SPINNING FASTER THAN THE LINE IS GOING OUT. AND I KEEP THE LINE OVER MY THUMB TO CONTROL THE LINE. IT ACTS AS A SORT OF TENSION DRAG. AS THE CAST GETS TO THE END I BRING MY LEFT-HAND UP TO THE ROD. AS THE BAIT ENTERS THE WATER I STOP THE REEL SPINNING

MR CRABTREE DROPS THE BAIT INTO THE CHUB SWIM THE OTHER SIDE OF THE RIVER

NOTHING DOING THERE TODAY, PETER. THE SWIM HASN'T BEEN BAITED UP LET'S GO UP TO THE ONE I HAVE BAITED

THIS IS OUR SWIM, PETER, IT'S ABOUT 6 FEET DEEP AND FULL OF CHUB UP TO 8lb IN WEIGHT. I'VE SET THE FLOAT AT 7 FEET SO THAT THE BAIT DRAGS BOTTOM

THESE WEEDS KEEP US OUT OF SIGHT OF THE FISH. YOU CAN'T BE TOO CAREFUL WITH THESE BIG CHUB. THEY LIE IN THIS BAY – JUST AT THE SLACK EDGE OF THE CURRENT

and like all chalk streams the water is excessively clear. You cannot fish close to your fish. You can see every detail in the water with wonderful clarity and the fish can see you equally wonderfully well. For swims close under the bank it is little good settling down immediately over them and fishing under the rod top. Long trotting is the only way. Post yourself upstream of the swim, some distance - thirty yards is not too much - and trot your tackle down to the swim.

Many good swims are away from the banks well out into mid-stream. For these long casting is necessary and Mr. Crabtree shows one way in which this may be done. This is another case of the need for adaptation on the part of the visiting angler. The typical roach rod of other streams will not make the long casts that are needed. The second of Mr. Crabtree's rods, already described, is the rod for this fishing. The spring and whip of the split cane middle and top joints will cast the heavy float tackle a long way once the trick of casting has been learnt. And this rod has the strength that it takes to manage these big fish. To play a five pound chub or a twelve pound

continued on page 16

About the chub

THE chub is a fish that on different occasions may seem anxious not to be caught, while on others it seems almost equally anxious to give itself up. The trout fisherman often has cause to curse the chub, for on some rivers on which the trout is the chief quarry, the chub is also present, in vast numbers. Again and again the trout fisherman will cast his fly or his minnow, and it will be taken, not by a trout but by a great blunt headed chub.

But get on to a river where the chub is an honoured resident, where many anglers seek him with all the cunning they have and he is a shy fish. On those rivers where we go specially to pursue him such as the Avon, he will test the skill of the finest angler.

The chub is above all a shoal fish. The smaller ones are not difficult to catch, but those above three pounds are different. The most extreme caution of approach must be used. Fine gut is necessary, but that is not so vital as keeping out of sight. You must fish from far off, trotting your tackle to them with the stream. They will take a bait on comparatively coarse gut that is long trotted to them more readily than they will take it on fine gut from close up.

No other fish is so ready to consider anything in the way of bait. They can be taken on worms, gentles, grubs, cheese, paste, frogs, flies, caterpillars, slugs, breadcrust, minnows, gudgeon, pith from the spinal cord of a bullock, elderberries, cherries, cubes of banana, and other things. The chub is a handsome, brassy-gleaming fish.

Chub

barbel thirty yards away from you, your tackle must not be too fragile.

Throughout its length the Avon is a splendid river, and anywhere on it the fisherman may be sure of having good sport and enjoying himself very much indeed. But for sheer size of fish, for the greatest chance of record beaters or at least glass casers, Christchurch is beyond comparison the best part of the river. It is only there that you will find those great barbel, and the average size of all fish is greater if recorded catches are any guide.

However, let no fisherman be kept away from the rest of the river by this fact. Anywhere that fishing tickets are to be had, the angler may be sure of a fine time on this lovely river. Apart from Christchurch, good centres are Ringwood, Fordingbridge and Downton.

It is not only the float fisherman that can have such fine sport. There is splendid fly fishing. The fly fisherman that goes after the chub with a dry fly may have the time of his life. And once above Christchurch, there are trout which though not present in very great numbers as they would be on a purely trout stream, do run to fine weights.

MR CRABTREE AND PETER HAVE STARTED TO FISH

LET IT WORK DOWN GRADUALLY WITH THE PULL OF THE STREAM. IF YOU CHECK IT THE FISH WILL BE SUSPICIOUS

THE TACKLE SWIMS DOWN SEVERAL TIMES WITHOUT RESULT ... THEN

THERE, PETER, HE'S ON!

OH, I HOPE YOU DON'T LOSE HIM!

IF HE'S WELL HOOKED WE WON'T LOSE HIM. THERE ARE THREE CAUSES FOR FISH THAT BREAK YOU— SNAGS, AND THERE ARE NONE HERE, BAD TACKLE, AND BAD FISHING

THE CRABTREES HAVE HOOKED A FISH

OUR FIRST AVON CHUB, PETER, AND A GOOD ONE! WE MUST PLAY IT CAREFULLY— THESE BIG CHUB FIGHT WELL AT THIS TIME OF THE YEAR—BETTER THAN THEY DO IN THE SUMMER

WHAT SO MANY BEGINNERS DON'T REALISE IS THAT YOU MUST KEEP YOUR ROD UP WHEN PLAYING A FISH. THE SPRING OF THE ROD ABSORBS THE PLUNGES OF THE FISH AND KEEPS THE STRAIN OFF YOUR FINE GUT

IF YOU DON'T USE FINE TACKLE, YOU WON'T HOOK THESE BIG OLD CHUB— BUT YOU MUST REMEMBER IT'S FINE AND LET YOUR ROD TAKE THE STRAIN

LET THE FISH RUN WHEN IT WANTS TO— AGAINST THE CHECK OF THE REEL. YOU CAN USE SENSITIVE FINGER PRESSURE ON THE EDGE OF THE REEL TOO. THIS REEL IS VERY SENSITIVE!

In winter this river is a pike spinner's dream. It is good spinning water well stocked with pike of high average size. It must be remembered however, that in some seasons spinning is not allowed at Christchurch because of the presence of salmon. In no season is it allowed there after Christmas.

Making a figure-of-eight knot.

NETS

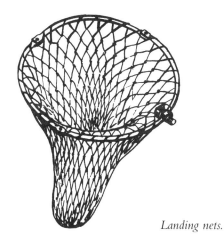

Landing nets.

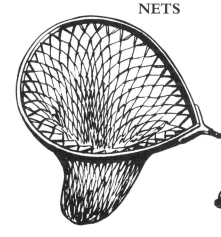

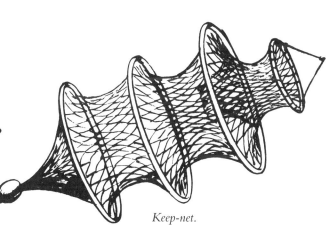

Keep-net.

To land his fish the fisherman will need a landing net. Fine gut that will play a fish will not lift it from the water. This net should be large and it should be strong. Sooner or later in the careers of most fishermen will come a day when a really big fish is hooked. If it is lost through the smallness or weakness of the landing net it is a tragedy. A keep-net is an essential so that fish may be retained alive and unhurt until the end of the day and then returned to the water as sound as they left it.

Fishing the slow river

TO come to a slow and gentle river, a river such as the great Ouse, after the Hampshire Avon, is a very great change. It is a change that must be reflected in methods and tackle. I will not say that it is a change to anything less enjoyable. Slow rivers will not yield you the huge specimens that are to be had in Hampshire, but nowhere in England will you find country more peaceful, more rural, more quietly forgotten seeming than that about the banks of these rivers. In Bedfordshire, in Huntingdonshire, in Suffolk and Rutland you may go with your rod and forget time. Nothing will seem real but this drowsy solitude in which you are lost.

Here will be not the fast heavy gin-clear water that you left in Hampshire, but a broad river that winds in easy curves through a flat or undulating country, loamy, richly farmed. Pollard willows will be much in evidence; were it summer the banks would in many places be thickly grown with rushes. There will be no bottom of golden scoured gravel, but easy gentle glides and deep quiet holes.

The fish population of this river will probably be rather different from that of the Avon. There will be no trout, no barbel, but the roach will be present. They will not have such a high average size, but they need not be small, and you may reasonably expect to get a really good fish from time to time.

The chub may or may not be present. Where it is, the size will not be anything like that of Hampshire. A three-pounder will be a good fish. Where the stream glides slowly under the willows or in the large almost still eddies should be the places to find them. And even on this river, so different in character from the Avon, one thing still holds good. Tempt your chub from a distance, do not try to fish right over them. In Avon or Ouse, they are shy fish.

The perch will be here, and here again the average size will be smaller. In fact, you may say that no species will be so big here as in Hampshire. Though there are many shoals with scarcely a fish above half-a-pound among them, in the deep holes and under the roots grandfathers do lurk. A deep cosy hole close to a shallow where the small fry play should be the place to find a good perch. However great his liking for the deeps, a perch must never be far from his food.

The pike will be here too. There will be many of them and with no obvious reason why they should not grow big. But in fact the majority do not reach any great size. Here and there one will grow to twenty pounds and more, but in general a ten pounder is a good fish. It seems that the greater purity of the water of such rivers as the Wye and the Avon makes this difference in the growth of pike.

However, the average fisherman is not likely to worry about this. If he can go out for a day with a reasonable chance of getting several pike, with one perhaps, on a good day, approaching ten pounds, he will be content.

Our slow river will probably hold a fish that was absent from the Avon, that is the bream. The bream is no fighter with strong currents. It being winter now it is unlikely that you will meet him, but should the weather be mild, he might turn up in your roach swim.

There is one feature of these slow rivers which should be a great pleasure to the fisherman. They are generally rich in mills. And is there anything more stimulating to the angler than a mill? The waters of a mill pool look so suggestive of fish, and indeed they are excellent places to fish. The great eddies at the side of a pool are fine places to look for perch. The biggest fish of a river will often come from its mill pools. And anyway there is a mystery and excitement about them as about no other part of the river.

THE CRABTREES HAVE GONE TO A RIVER WITH A SLOW AND GENTLE FLOW — NOT FAST AND HEAVY LIKE THE HAMPSHIRE AVON — THEY ARE AFTER ROACH

WE MUST FISH MUCH FINER HERE, PETER, THAN WE DID ON THE AVON

THERE WE HAD TO USE PLENTY OF LEAD TO GET THE BAIT DOWN TO THE FISH — HERE THE FISH HAVE TIME TO LOOK CLOSER, SO WE'LL USE A 6x CAST AND A No 14 HOOK-TO-GUT, A LIGHT FLOAT AND 4 SHOT

THIS IS THE ROD I LIKE FOR ROACHING ON THIS SORT OF RIVER — 11 FT LONG, 3 JOINTS — BOTTOM AND MIDDLE WHOLE CANE, AND TOP JOINT SPLIT CANE

WE'LL USE THE REEL WE USED BEFORE — YOU CAN'T BEAT THIS TYPE

38

AND HERE'S OUR SWIM. NEAR THE BANK THERE'S A DEEPISH CHANNEL WITH A GENTLE CURRENT THROUGH IT — A GOOD PLACE FOR ROACH

Bernard Venables

THE CRABTREES ARE FISHING A SLOW RIVER FOR ROACH

FIRST, PETER, WE MUST PLUMB THE DEPTH TO FIND HOW TO SET OUR FLOAT. SEE HOW THE POINT OF THE HOOK IS STUCK LIGHTLY INTO THE CORK IN THE PLUMMET

39

WE LOWER THE PLUMMET QUIETLY INTO THE WATER. SEE — THE FLOAT'S SET TOO HIGH. WE MUST PUT IT DOWN A BIT. WE WANT THE BAIT JUST OFF THE BOTTOM

THAT'S BETTER, JUST THE TIP SHOWING

WHEN WE TAKE OFF THE PLUMMET, THE HOOK JUST CLEARS THE BOTTOM

FOR BAIT WE'RE GOING TO USE THE GENTLES WE BOUGHT AT THE TACKLE SHOP. SO I THROW IN A FEW A YARD OR TWO UPSTREAM OF OUR SWIM. THEY'LL REACH THE BOTTOM IN THE SWIM, AND INTEREST THE FISH AND MAKE THEM LOOK FOR MORE

Bernard Venables

NOW WE PUT TWO ON THE HOOK — JUST KNICKED UNDER THE SKIN AT THE THICK END — LIKE THIS

In fishing this river the Crabtrees have one thing less to worry about and one thing more. The problem of getting the bait down to the fish before it was swept out of the swim has gone. But now they have to consider the fact that in this slow current the fish can examine the bait at their leisure. The tackle that they used on the Avon would scare every fish out of the swim at once if they used it here. Everything must be finer and lighter.

The rod is different too. That which they used on the Avon would be much too slow in its response for this fishing. A quick steely action is needed. The Avon fishing was far off. This is not.

Here it is a good method to fish close to the rod top, using the same length of line all the time. On the Avon, roach had to take a good gulp at the bait to get it at all. That made the float dip sharply and decisively, and the lightning strike was not essential. But here roach can play delicately with the bait, sucking it in and rejecting it in a moment. Many of these bites will not show as a real dip of the float at all. Often it will be no more than a quiver, a slight sideways movement, or a barely perceptible pause. The response of the fisherman must be instantaneous if he is not to miss his fish.

The method that the Crabtrees are using is, of course, far from being the only one that can be used on this type of river. Even within this method they have quite a wide choice of baits. In addition to the gentles they are using, they could use small red worms, the tail of a lobworm, paste, breadcrust or stewed wheat. And that is not the end of them. But besides their float fishing they could ledger in the deep holes; they could float ledger, or they could paternoster for the perch.

Spinning for perch on this river at this time of the year could give good sport. In the summer it would be impossible, so thick is the weed growth, but now this has died down. The threadline outfit would be the tackle to use.

Spinning also suggests the pike, and this is excellent water for it. But that and spinning for perch need not be dealt with here. Later in this book we shall accompany Mr. Crabtree and Peter on expeditions for both these methods. We shall in fact be going piking with them very soon, for it is getting towards the end of the season, and there is no time for pike like the back end.

PIKE *the back-end is the time for big fish*

YES, the back-end is the time for big fish. That is one of the most certainly true things that can be said about pike fishing. Pike are uncertain fish about which it is difficult to prophesy. It is impossible to say in advance that this will be a good day or this will not be a good day. It can be said that this looks as if it ought to be a good day, and quite often it will turn out so; and an apparently bad day will generally prove to be so. But there are many exceptions, so many that prophesying about pike fishing is a most unrewarding occupation. But this can be said, that for big fish there is no time like the end of the season. 'December good, January better, February best' runs the saying, and all experience bears this out.

It is not only that the big fish seem more ready to take a bait towards the end of the season. A big fish is sometimes caught as early as October. But the big fish themselves are bigger in the last months of the season. The pike is a fish that suffers heavily from the effects of spawning, and is long in recovering. The coming of autumn sees it still lank and ill-conditioned, weakly and hollow-bellied. But about October improvement commences and continues throughout November and December, so that by the turn of the year the pike is a different creature, firm now, deep in the body, and full of savage energy. The increase in weight resulting from this can be quite considerable.

Weight is also increased by another factor. All these big pike are females, and in the last two or three months of the season they are ripening for the business of spawning. When you consider that the eggs of a ripe female pike of 32 lb will weigh 5 lb, you will realise how big a difference this can make.

Anyway, whatever the cause, it is an undoubted fact that the greater proportion of the biggest pike have been caught in the last three months of the season. And on those occasions when I have seen a big pike caught early in the season, say in October, my feeling has been, what a pity, if it had been caught a couple of months later it would have been several pounds heavier. For on every occasion it has been plain in the lean flanks and flabby keel of the fish that it had not come to its best.

But apart from the question of size and the possibility of taking specimen fish, fishing for pike in the last months is incomparably better sport than it is earlier. The unrecovered pike is a poor creature with no spirit to fight the pull of a line. Too often it can be dragged in with scarcely a wag. But meet that same fish in February!

The Crabtrees prepare to start on their first day's pike fishing.

OF all the fishermen who fish for pike, the majority fish for them by live-baiting. Whether it or spinning is the better method is a thing about which fishermen will always argue, but never settle. Devotees of live-baiting claim that their method gets bigger fish, but for the spinner it must be pointed out that in fact many of the biggest fish have been taken spinning. The truth is, I think, that big fish may be had either way.

The spinners claim that their way is more active, and this is true and an advantage in cold weather. But the quietude of live-baiting is a large part of its attraction to many people. It is largely a question of mood. On some days the quietness of sitting watching the big float is very delightful. It is a quietness shot with a particularly thrilling excitement. You watch the float bobbing slightly with the movement of the bait. You see it move this way and that in small spasmodic movements. It takes little teetering trips in towards the reeds and away from them. You watch in stillness, held in a long fascination, expecting every moment to see the movements quicken with a sudden agitation. You may soon perceive that at one place a special alarm comes to the float every time it drifts there. Then at each fresh arrival at this spot, your heart will be in your mouth and your hand tremble with expectancy. For these sudden alarms tell you that in that vicinity there is a pike.

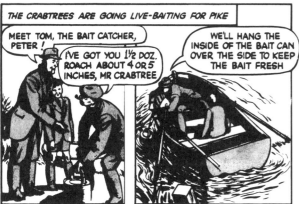

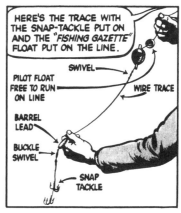

Then will come a moment when an extra movement comes to the float, a sharper, stronger, more prolonged movement than the bait could give. The float may slide across the water and then go quietly under.

Now you must wait a little while, giving line while the heavy unseen force beneath the surface tows your tackle with it. There is a risk that if you strike too soon, before your pike has turned the bait in its mouth, you will snatch the hooks from its mouth without their securing a hold. So wait then, and you may feel a jerk as the bait is turned. Now is the time to strike, but be sure you do it the right way. The strike should not be a sharp jerk, it

should be a steady, heavy draw. And in making it you should remember that the pike has a very bony mouth, which offers only certain places for a hook hold. These are mostly round the side of the mouth. The roof is hard, bony and impenetrable. Hooks pulled against it will slide off. Let your strike, therefore, be more or less parallel with the water surface and in a direction opposite to that in which the fish is moving. Even when you have remembered all this, you will always find that you lose a certain number of fish through the hooks coming away before you can use the gaff. But assuming that all is well and your fish is firmly hooked, do not try to drag it straight out.

The pike is a heavy fish and must be allowed to run if it wants to. Slip on the check of your reel so that the fish runs against some resistance. More strain can be used when necessary by finger pressure on the edge of the drum of the reel.

While you should let the fish have its head if it is of any size, there is no need to play it too lightly. If your tackle is as sound as it should be, you can make the fish fight for all the line it gains.

But in the case of a very heavy fish, twenty pounds or upwards, you must be cautious. Do not be too anxious to put on heavy strain. If you are holding the fish hard and it makes a sudden plunge, it may break you. These very big fish can usually be told as soon as they are hooked. You do not at once feel the savage tugs and twists that you feel with the middle sized fish. The big fish feels at first like a heavy immovable weight, so much so that you may think that you have hooked the bottom. Then when it starts to run, the run will be ponderous and irresistible. The angler then who tries to hold his fish will be asking for trouble and will get it. The bigger the fish, the more this is so.

Do not be led by stories of immense pike into using tackle that is too heavy. For most pike fishing, a line of twelve pounds breaking strain is all you need. Big fish have been landed on lighter lines. But too light a line is a risk and 12 lb. breaking strain may be regarded as about right. The only exception is where you are fishing for a particular fish which is known to be very heavy, and which lies in a place surrounded by snags. Then you will be wise to use a really heavy line. I remember a very big fish indeed that I hooked in a bay flanked on both sides by tree roots that ran down into the water. I did not know of this fish in advance and was fishing with an 11 lb. line. The fish made one run out into the river and then turned and ran for the roots. I had no choice but to try to hold it.

The strain was too much and the line parted with a crack like a pistol shot. An event like that leaves a scar on your memory.

When at last you have done everything right and the fish is brought to the bank, you must gaff it. Here again caution is necessary. Wild swipes with the gaff will be fatal. Wait until you can draw the fish in quietly with no kicks left, and then draw in the gaff smoothly under the chin. This is the only proper place to use the gaff. With the same steady movement draw the fish ashore. And take it well back from the bank so that it may not flap back into the water.

WELL, PETER, WE'VE HAD A DAY'S LIVE-BAITING, NOW WE'LL SEE HOW WE GET ON SPINNING FOR PIKE ON A RIVER. I THINK IT'S A MORE INTERESTING METHOD, AND IT KEEPS YOU WARMER!

MR Crabtree and Peter are now going pike fishing by a method which, though it has not so many disciples as live-baiting, is much more firmly believed in by its followers. And I think rightly so. Live-baiting is a very pleasant method, but taking it all round, spinning has much more to offer the fisherman. To begin with he is much more constantly occupied, which is a consideration when winter weather has a nip in it. But there is more to it than that. The live-baiter chooses his place, casts out his bait, and then waits for the pike to come to him. The spinner, on the other hand, is all the time testing his skill and knowledge. He is always searching the places that his water knowledge tells him should hold pike; probing here and there, constantly doing something, seeking the quarry in every foot of likely water. And all the time he is building up further his knowledge of the ways of pike.

And though skill enters into live-baiting, it does not do so to anything like the extent it does into spinning. The spinner drops his bait into every hole and corner, searching out fish from places not practical for the live-baiter. He does not wait for the pike to be tempted out of his quiet hole, he puts his bait in there to him.

IN FACT I THINK IT'S THE BEST OF ALL WINTER FISHING!

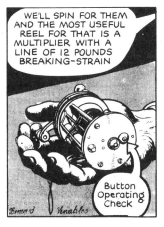

WE'LL SPIN FOR THEM AND THE MOST USEFUL REEL FOR THAT IS A MULTIPLIER WITH A LINE OF 12 POUNDS BREAKING-STRAIN

Button Operating Check

MR CRABTREE AND PETER HAVE REACHED THE RIVER ON THEIR FIRST DAY'S PIKE FISHING

SEE, PETER, I PUT THE MULTIPLYING REEL ON TOP OF THE ROD WITH THE HANDLES TO THE RIGHT

THIS ROD IS SPLIT CANE AND 7 FT. LONG. BUT IT COULD BE GREENHEART, AND EITHER LONGER OR SHORTER. THE MAIN THING IS TO HAVE IT FAIRLY SPRINGY RIGHT DOWN TO THE BUTT

WE ATTACH THE WIRE TRACE TO THE END OF THE LINE. DO YOU SEE THE SWIVEL AT THE TOP AND THE SPRING LINK AT THE BOTTOM?

HERE'S A GOOD BAIT TO TRY FIRST— A KIDNEY SPOON. PUT IT ON THE SPRING LINK

WHEN WE DRAW IT THROUGH THE WATER THE SPOON REVOLVES ROUND THE LEADED BAR AND FLASHES LIKE A SMALL TURNING FISH

THOSE ARE THE SPOTS TO GO FOR, PETER!

Current →

NOW THE CRABTREES LOOK AT THE RIVER FOR LIKELY PLACES FOR PIKE

2

THE CRABTREES WORK DOWN THE RIVER TRYING THE LIKELY PLACES TILL—

TURN YOUR HAND OVER WHEN YOU CAST SO THAT THE PALM FACES FORWARD. AIM HIGH OR YOU WILL JUST HIT THE WATER AT YOUR FEET. CONTROL THE SPOOL OF THE REEL WITH YOUR THUMB

CAST DOWN-STREAM OR DOWN-STREAM AND ACROSS

THIS LOOKS A GOOD PLACE— I'LL LET THE BAIT SINK DEEP AND WIND IT BACK AS SLOWLY AS I CAN. YOU CAN'T BE TOO SLOW AS LONG AS YOU KEEP IT OFF THE BOTTOM

BELOW THE SURFACE—

STRIKE!

3

Many a pike not hungry enough to come out to a bait, is caught on the spinning bait he can grab as it swims past his head. The spinner develops a high degree of accuracy in the casting of his baits. He must do so if he is to get the best that spinning can offer. And when his bait is cast he must work it with skill and knowledge. He must spin it at such a depth that it is low in the water, down to the pike, yet does not foul the bottom. Sometimes he cannot avoid this. Every spinner loses a bait on occasions. Then he must spin it at the right speed. Unless he is very hungry, a pike will not go to great trouble to grab a bait.

The bait that is easy to grab will always be more alluring to him than one that is not. So the spinner must spin slowly. If he can make his bait limp a little, so much the better. The golden rule in pike spinning is spin deeply and spin slowly.

Even the most confirmed live-baiter will usually admit that spinning catches more pike. But, he says, it does not catch such big pike. Only a very little scrutiny of pike records is needed to disprove this. In the past season, the pike that won the Daily Mirror prize rod for pike was one of $35\frac{1}{2}$ lb., a magnificent fish, that was taken spinning by Mr. A. Jackson. He was using a spoon.

In 1920 a pike of 53 lb. was caught by Mr. John Garvin in Lough Conn, and on the same day he had another of 30 lb. He was using a 2 inch spoon. A fish that for many years shared the British record with another, weighed 37 lb. It was caught spinning with an artificial minnow in the Wye. I once witnessed and had the pleasure of gaffing a pike of 30 lb. taken spinning with a 2 inch spoon. To these fish could be added many more. But just these few do show, I think, that big fish can be as well taken spinning as by live-baiting.

A fisherman may sometimes go to a water and there have an excellent day with the pike. At the first opportunity he will hasten back expecting to repeat his success. Too often he will, on the contrary, have only a poor day the second time. And there we have one of the most characteristic things about pike. They are very unpredictable. One day a lake may seem stuffed with pike all just waiting for your bait to be thrown in to grab it. Another day you might almost believe that the same lake had not a pike in it. It is all a matter of the stage of a pike's hunger. For his appetite runs in a cycle. At its peak he will take almost anything. A dead fish thrown in on the end of a line and merely allowed to sink to the bottom may take a pike then. At the other extreme nothing can interest him.

A bait may be dangled over his nose and he will stare through it. Then there are the stages in between when a pike is hungry to some extent, but it rests with the angler's skill to induce the fish to take. That is how it goes on the average day's pike fishing. Be lucky enough to catch the pike at the peak of his hunger, and you may have a red-letter day.

It is this, too, which explains the difficulty of predicting by the weather what pike fishing will be like on a given day. Catch the fish somewhere near the middle of their feeding cycle, and you may judge by the weather what the prospects are. But be by the water at the top of the pike's hunger and you may have good sport on the most hopeless-looking day. Alternatively, get it at the lowest ebb of its hunger and you may not get a fish on the most perfect-looking fishing day you ever saw.

What then is good weather for pike fishing? Traditionally good pike weather is the hard frosty day when you must constantly suck the rings of your rod to dissolve the ice from them. But here tradition is very wrong. The best of all weathers for pike is the dull, overcast, mild day that comes in winter. If it is slightly drizzly it seems to help rather than the reverse.

Pike can be caught in severe frosty weather, but I have never known really good days to be had then. When there has been a prolonged period of frost, and then warmer weather comes, about three days after the ice goes, the sport may be very good.

The truth is that while the weather is severe, pike, like so many fish, become a little torpid, and cease to feed. Consequently when warmer weather comes they are hungry, and feed greedily.

It always grieves me to see anglers fishing for pike during the summer. A pike is only a poor thing then, still exhausted from spawning. If it is hooked it cannot fight as it should. Pike should be left alone until October. They should be given a chance to recover. To hook them then and return them to the water will do them no harm. And if they are big, they are more worth keeping. Who could want to keep a poor flabby creature that has no fight in it and can only look ugly in a glass case? At the same time many pike are kept which are much too small. Size limits for pike on most fisheries are much too low. What is the object of killing a pike if it is not to go into a glass case. And no prize is good enough for a glass case under twenty pounds.

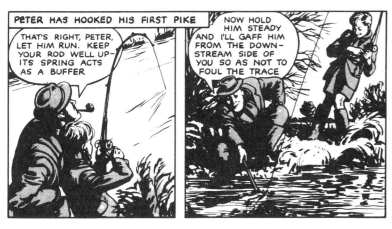

Here is more of Mr. Crabtree's pike tackle

GILDEX   GRANGECASTER

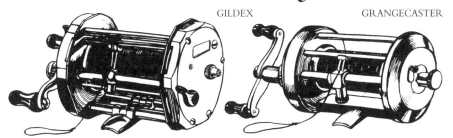

OTHER REELS

Mr. Crabtree uses a multiplying reel for spinning, and there is no doubt that this is the best kind for all but very light spinning. Some fishermen still prefer a centre-pin reel, and of this type there is nothing to beat the Aerial (p8). The disadvantage is however, that it will not cast baits much under an ounce. A multiplier will cast baits of half-an-ounce and a little less. Here are two multipliers which are good. Both have a level-wind mechanism which spreads the line evenly on the spool.

ARTIFICIAL BAITS

A   B   C   D   E   F

The first of the baits shown here, A, the 'Pliquatic' bait is not really an artificial bait at all. It is an actual fish enclosed in a flexible, transparent skin. The bait feels soft to the pike and therefore life-like, but his teeth cannot penetrate it. This is a very good bait. B is a spoon, an old favourite. C is a wagtail. D is the Hardy spoon. E is the 'Silver Devon' spoon. F is a spoon Mr. Crabtree has made himself and is 8 in. long. It was suggested by the Hardy spoon and the Silver Devon spoon. The non-spinning head is sheet metal instead of lead, as in the Hardy spoon, to reduce weight in this large size. It is meant for big fish in deep water.

DEAD-BAIT FLIGHTS

A   B   C   D

To spin with a dead natural fish such as dace, or gudgeon, it must be mounted on a flight. To use A and B push the pin down gullet of bait and spike hooks to side. With C, the lower single hook gives a curve to the tail of bait, upper one goes through lips, spike goes into side. With D, wire on hook is threaded with baiting needle from vent to tail. Gives slow rolling spin.

ANTI-KINK LEADS

These are put on the line just above top swivel of trace to stop spinning of bait passing up line and causing kinking. Those shown are all of type that can be put on without untying line from trace.

A   B   C   D

33

Now Peter is going to learn plug fishing, the most sporting way of all for pike.

JUST as spinning may be said to be superior to live-baiting, in its greater interest and scope for initiative, so plug fishing, which is a sort of offshoot of spinning, can claim to be better than spinning. All the virtues that spinning has, plug fishing has too, but developed further. The accuracy that is so characteristic of spinning is present in plug fishing even more finely developed. There is scarcely a space in the reeds, an opening under the over-hanging trees that is too small to have a plug popped into it. To get the best of this accuracy and handiness, the appropriate outfit should be used with plugs. They can be cast with various rods and reels, but not to get the best out of them. It is not uncommon to see them being fished on a threadline outfit. This is a horrible mixture of ingredients that must result in a high percentage of losses of fish or losses of plugs or both. The threadline reel with its fine line is designed to cast very light baits, and that is its only justification. This fine line cannot properly set the big hooks with which plugs are usually armed. Either the hooks do not go in over the barb and the fish kicks off, or in the effort to set them in, the line breaks. Even the strain of continual casting of such a big bait will finally break the line.

The only proper reel for plugs is the multiplier. It was for this fishing that the reel was developed, though it is now used successfully for other purposes as well.

The rod that was designed specially for plug fishing is the short bait caster with the offset reel-seating, generally five feet in length. This outfit fits so easily to the hand that it seems like an extension of the arm. The bait can be almost pointed into the places it is meant to go. A braided silk or nylon line of 12 lb. is best. The trace should be about six inches long, of wire, with one swivel at the top and a link or snap swivel at the bottom.

That is the standard plug outfit. In practice there are many occasions when I vary it by using a ten foot spinning rod. On rivers for instance, where the banks are high, or bushes or reeds are much about the banks, the longer rod gives you the extra reach which is often necessary. The short rod is most suited to boat fishing.

In the plugs themselves there is an enormous variety, which lend themselves to an even larger variety of ways of using them. The Crabtrees are using a floating and diving plug. With this alone there is an endless number of ways of working it. For each problem in the course of a day's fishing the bait provides a different answer. It is never a mere matter of casting out and reeling in. Each cast is a matter of experiment and different exploitation of the bait's possibilities.

35

Then as well as the innumerable patterns of this type, there is the plug that does not dive but is worked entirely on the surface. There are various patterns of this kind, and think how useful they can be in those shallow waters which abound with pike but are thick with weed almost to the surface, even in the winter. These are good baits for warmish days, and exciting it is to use them. Sometimes a pike will come with such dash that it will miss the bait, flinging it a foot out of the water.

There are plugs for deep water too. There are plugs for every sort of water. There are plugs which sink slowly, not so fast as a spoon does. There are plugs which sink faster and go deeper, the baits to use in deep lakes. In fact there is a plug to fish at every level. On the surface, just below it, then so on at every depth to the deepest. And at all levels it is a bait that wriggles and swims in a way far too fishlike for any hungry pike to resist.

It is in America that the plug has really been developed in its greatest variety. At the moment of writing it is only slowly that the scope of plug production is widening in England. But I think the fisherman can look forward to a steadily greater choice from the British makers.

PLUGS *here are some of the patterns Mr. Crabtree uses*

Before the war a very great variety of plugs could be bought in England. Almost all of these were imported from America and had a very high standard of finish and ingenuity. There was a plug for every possible purpose, depth and state of water. Import ceased with the war and for a long time the plug fisher was dependent on what he could make for himself. Now however, good British plugs are appearing on the market, and undoubtedly the supply and variety of these will increase. To give some idea of the variety of which plugs are capable I am showing here a number of American patterns as well as English ones. I have

reason to believe that by the time this book is published, the range of British patterns available will be very much wider.

The patterns shown on the top row are all British. The first two are floaters that can be worked at any depth from just sub-surface to deep according to the force and continuity of the wind in. In action they have a very injured look. The third one is a semi-transparent floater that dives fairly deep when wound in. The last one is also semi-transparent and a slow sinker that dives and wriggles as it is recovered. A good deep water bait.

The second row are all American and floaters. The first one is a shallow diver with a very enticing wriggle. I have caught more pike on it than any other bait.

The second one is a deep diver and very good. The third one is the unjointed form of the first one, in a colouration for dark days and coloured water.

The patterns on the bottom row are all American and all surface baits. There are days, early in the season, about October, and again at the end of the season, when they can be very useful indeed. When the weather is warm pike are apt to lie in shallow water, quite often where the weeds come almost to the surface. Then these surface baits may be very deadly. The first one, which is the best, should not be wound straight in, the speed should be varied, sometimes

stopping, sometimes giving little spurts. It is astonishingly like a creature, injured, and struggling to dive.

The second bait has a spinning head and appears like a mouse fussing across the surface. The third one is a popping bait. It is cast into openings in the weeds that come to the surface, and worked with sudden jerks that throw up a small spout of spray with a distinct pop

SPRING

IN spring comes a big change in the fisherman's year. And if he is an all-round fisherman, one who fishes for trout, there comes too the cream of his year. Gone are the days of pike fishing and roach fishing among the seered and yellow reeds, spring is here. And here as well are trout, the angler's finest quarry. From the season's opening onwards he will be having his most delectable fishing through the months of the river's tenderest beauty. All parts of the year have their magic for the fisherman, but he who puts away his rods till coarse fishing starts again is missing a great deal. He is missing the very best of the fisherman's year.

Of course for many fishermen this is unavoidable. If there is no trout fishing to be had in your locality, there is nothing you can do about it. But if trout fishing is by any means to be had, take it. It is the angler's ultimate pleasure.

Everything that makes the fisherman's hours lovely is now more evident than at any other time. First as he fishes the primroses will bloom about him. The milkmaids will cluster on the banks and the anemones will blow in the spinneys. Early days of warmth will bring the first bees about the pussy willow. Then April will melt into May and a sea of blue will wash out from the trees and down the banks. It will be bluebell time. For a little while there will be an ascendancy of blue. Speedwell and bugle and other small plants will be about the fisherman. But as the month draws on towards June there will be a sudden gush of bloom over the trees. The hawthorn and the chestnut will bloom, the rowan and the wayfaring tree, and minor things besides. This

Brown Trout

The season of the fly-fisher

is spring's loveliest moment and the peak of the fisherman's year.

And the fishing that he does now will be in the same spirit. The trout that he angles for is the most beautiful and high mettled fish that swims in our waters. It is a fish hard to hook and when hooked most uncertain in the landing. A trout of a pound weight hooked in a mountain or moorland stream will give you some of the intensest moments of your life before it is brought to the net - if you do succeed in bringing it thus far.

As is fitting, the methods and tackle that you will use are equally fine. You will carry very little with you. You will not use groundbait, you will have no gentles, no worms, no pastes, no concoctions of any kind. All you will carry in your bag is a box of flies, tiny gossamer things, a cast case and a damper. You will

have somewhere on your person too, a small pair of scissors, and, if you are fishing dry fly, a little bottle of oil to oil your fly. With just this and the whole day before you in May or early June, life has nothing more to offer. You can be a completely happy man.

At no other time in the angler's calendar is time less felt. The long day slips by with no consciousness of things other than this river bank can offer. The birds sing, the insects hum in the grasses, and the warm breeze lifts softly in the angler's hair. Time has ceased for him and nothing is more urgent than his leisurely stalking of the trout that rises under the opposite bank. Only when the sun begins to slant on the water does he know the day has almost gone and it will soon be time for the evening rise.

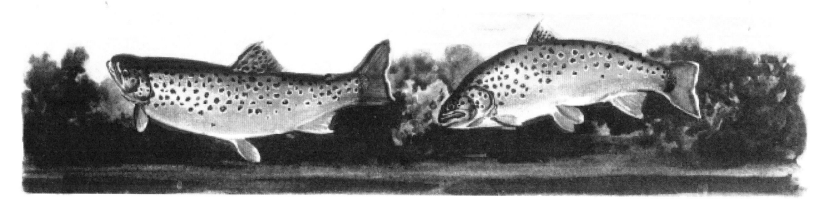

Brown Trout

Spring has come, so Peter is going to have his first lesson in fly fishing.

YES, PETER, IT'S A LOVELY SPRING MORNING— JUST THE DAY TO GO FLY-FISHING, AND THAT, IN MY OPINION IS THE MOST DELIGHTFUL OF ALL FORMS OF FISHING!

Now here the Crabtrees are going dry fly fishing, and the first thing I must tell you is that this river they are fishing is by no means typical of all rivers on which the dry fly may be used. Conditions do vary very much on rivers of different types. This river of theirs is of the sort where the dry fly is used more than anything else. It is a river of smooth and even flow, where even the sharp and shallow runs are not rough as compared with, for instance, the Devonshire rivers. Its water is almost as clear as air. Both fish and man can see very clearly in it. It has a luxuriant weed growth, which in turn means that there is much fly life. As a result trout are much more ready to expect flies to come floating to them. On almost every day there are regular rises to fly - a thing unknown on many rivers. And since there is always this abundant supply of flies on which they may feed, and the water is so clear, trout are not easy to deceive. They can inspect any fly closely before taking it. If they are at all suspicious of it they leave it. There are plenty more. A fisherman who can catch trout with a dry fly on this river should be able to adapt himself to rivers of other types. This might be said to be the prototype of dry fly fishing.

This river is a chalk stream. That is to say it has its origin in the chalk hills. The rain that feeds it does not come straight into it as it does in so many rivers, causing floods and heavy water. First the rain seeps deep down into the chalk. Then it emerges again as a

WELL, PETER, YOU'RE GOING TO LEARN TO CAST A FLY, AND THE SECRET OF IT IS AN EASY FLOWING RHYTHM

WE'LL START ON THIS POND SO THAT THERE WILL BE NO CURRENT TO BOTHER YOU

42

THIS IS THE ROD—9' LONG —SPLIT CANE— COULD BE GREENHEART, AND IT HAS AN EASY SPRINGY ACTION DOWN TO THE BUTT, BUT IT'S NOT SLOPPY

AND THIS IS A FLY REEL, THERE ARE MANY TYPES, BUT ALMOST ANY REEL WILL DO AT A PINCH!

Bernard Venables

THERE ARE TWO MAIN TYPES OF LINE— DOUBLE TAPERED AND BALANCED. THE BALANCED LINE MAKES CASTING EASIER. BOTH ARE HEAVY TO MAKE THE ROD WORK, AND MAKE IT POSSIBLE TO CAST INTO WIND. IF A LINE IS TOO LIGHT THE ROD WON'T WORK PROPERLY— IF IT'S TOO HEAVY IT WILL MAKE THE ROD SEEM WEAK. SIZE Nº 2 SUITS MOST RODS

DIAGRAM OF DOUBLE-TAPERED LINE

FORWARD END OF LINE

DIAGRAM OF BALANCED LINE

(THESE DIAGRAMS ARE GREATLY EXAGGERATED)

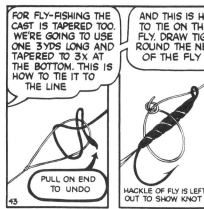

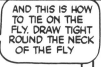

FOR FLY-FISHING THE CAST IS TAPERED TOO. WE'RE GOING TO USE ONE 3YDS LONG AND TAPERED TO 3X AT THE BOTTOM. THIS IS HOW TO TIE IT TO THE LINE

PULL ON END TO UNDO

AND THIS IS HOW TO TIE ON THE FLY. DRAW TIGHT ROUND THE NECK OF THE FLY

HACKLE OF FLY IS LEFT OUT TO SHOW KNOT

NOW HOLD THE ROD LOOSELY IN YOUR HAND. DON'T GRIP IT TIGHTLY, YOUR HAND IS JUST A PIVOT— IT'S THE ROD THAT DRIVES THE LINE

DRAW ABOUT 10 YDS OF LINE FROM THE REEL AND GET IT OUT IN FRONT OF YOU BY SWITCHING THE ROD LIKE A WHIP. NOW YOU'RE READY TO START

FOLLOW THROUGH   PAUSE   PAUSE

START RAISING THE ROD FROM 1, QUICKENING SMOOTHLY INTO A BACKWARD FLIP OF ROD TOP AS IT NEARS THE VERTICAL. DON'T LET THE ROD GO PAST THE VERTICAL— USE YOUR THUMB AS A STOP! PAUSE WHILE THE LINE EXTENDS BEHIND YOU — THE LONGER THE LINE THE LONGER THE PAUSE. THEN START TO BRING THE ROD FORWARD, QUICKENING SMOOTHLY INTO A FLIP OF THE TOP AT 4 — PAUSE WHILE THE LINE FLIES OUT IN FRONT, AND FOLLOW THROUGH GENTLY. DON'T USE FORCE, DO IT SLOWLY. LET THE ROD DO THE WORK. AIM AT A SPOT A FOOT ABOVE THE WATER SO THAT YOUR FLY FALLS SOFTLY

clear spring which is the source of a river - a chalk stream. The result of this is that on a chalk stream there is always this clear and pellucid water. No flood or dirty water ever comes to trouble it. However great the rainfall, it is first filtered through the chalk hills. Though the river will vary in its height to some extent, it will not go to extremes. A clear clean river can be depended upon.

Now there are few of us who may have the chance to fish these lovely chalk streams. They are few and expensive. But the lessons that we learn by watching the Crabtrees fishing can be applied anywhere. If on another river, the Teme, the Severn, the Wharfe, or any of the many other rivers that hold trout, there is a rise to fly, we shall know what to do. But, of course, a great deal of the time there will not be a general rise. An odd fish here and there perhaps, and this can be cast to in the same way as if it were a chalk stream fish. But much of the time you will be put to it to find a rising fish. Then you apply the knowledge the fisherman gets to have of where trout lie. You will say to yourself 'There is a place where a trout should be. It has all that a trout needs for comfort. That rock or that shoulder of bank gives it shelter from the force of the current, but it is right against the current which will bring its food to it.'

So you cast your fly and let it float over the place that your reason tells you should hold a trout. Quite often there will be a trout there which will rise to your fly. Thus you can work all the way up the water, trying every place that you think might hold a trout. And the more of this you do, the more will you come to know of where trout are to be found.

The guiding rule is shelter from the current and proximity to the food that is brought down by the current. Behind rocks, just at the edge of the main current where it meets the slacker water. Where the current cuts in under the bank is often good. The flow of food is concentrated by the current and the trout wait for it in the little unevennesses in the bank and behind the stones on the bottom. Good too is the last of a glassy glide, just before the water tumbles in a rough stickle into the pool below. Then attention should be given to eddies beside the main current. A trout will generally lie just where the water turns into the eddy. Experience will show you many other places.

On these rougher, more rocky streams, choice of fly does not have to be the precise thing it is on the chalk stream. Here there is no such abundant fly life to pamper the fish. Flies do not

PETER HAS BEEN PRACTISING HIS CASTING AND CAN NOW CAST A FAIR LINE. HE AND MR CRABTREE ARE NOW GOING TO HAVE A DAY ON A TROUT STREAM

47

WE ARE GOING TO FISH DRY FLY, SO I'VE GREASED THE LINE TO MAKE IT FLOAT. WE'LL TIE ON A DRY FLY AND OIL IT TO MAKE IT FLOAT TOO. THE FLY IS A GREENWELL'S GLORY WHICH IS ABOUT AS GOOD A GENERAL FLY AS THERE IS

LOOK, PETER, THERE'S A FISH RISING TO FLIES AS THEY FLOAT DOWN. KNEEL TO KEEP OUT OF SIGHT AND START GETTING OUT LINE

PETER CASTS BACK AND FORTH IN THE AIR AS HE PULLS LINE FROM THE REEL AND SHOOTS IT TILL HE HAS ENOUGH TO REACH THE TROUT. THIS IS CALLED FALSE CASTING. IT SHOULD ALSO BE DONE BETWEEN PROPER CASTS TO DRY THE FLY

RIGHT, PETER, NOW LET YOUR FLY FALL ABOUT A FOOT UPSTREAM OF WHERE THE FISH ROSE AND A LITTLE TO THIS SIDE OF IT

PETER WAITS WHILE THE FLY FLOATS DOWN TO THE TROUT WHICH RISES AND TAKES THE FLY

STRIKE! — AH, YOU STRUCK TOO QUICKLY AND TOO HARD, BEFORE THE FISH HAD TURNED DOWN AGAIN!

YOU SNATCHED THE FLY OUT OF ITS MOUTH!

DRY THE FLY ON A PIECE OF AMADOU OR YOUR HANDKERCHIEF AND RE-OIL IT!

THAT FISH WON'T RISE AGAIN FOR A TIME — YOU'VE PUT IT DOWN!

BUT LOOK, THERE'S ANOTHER ONE!

48

come to them in orderly droves. When they do come they must be seized without any too particular inspection. To hesitate is to lose the fly. So flies that are a fair general suggestion of the natural flies will do very well. Greenwell's Glory, Gold-ribbed Hare's Ear, Tup's Indispensable and Pheasant Tail are good flies. There are as well various fancy flies which do not represent any natural fly. These are often very successful on these rivers. On the chalk stream there is no need for them. The proper imitation of the natural fly is more appropriate. But on these rougher streams such flies as Red Tag, Wickham's Fancy, Soldier Palmer, can be very useful indeed. And the Alder, though an imitation of a nat-

ural fly that appears in May, can be very useful to the fisherman all through the season. The same applies to the March Brown. One or two patterns of sedge will also serve the angler well.

In fishing his dry fly on a rocky river, the angler must, of course, stick to the smoother water. To fish the rougher water the wet fly is needed.

Now wherever the fly fisherman fishes, the basis of his sport is the natural flies on which the trout feed. They take his fly because they are looking for real flies. So it is easy to see that some sort of knowledge of the natural flies and their life history is a help to the fisherman.

On the chalk stream it is vital, and on many rivers it will make all the difference to the season's results. What then, are these flies?

The most important family of flies to the angler is that known as the *Ephemeridæ*. They are dainty creatures which when at rest, fold their wings over their bodies rather in the fashion of butterflies, hence they are known as upwinged flies. The fisherman is concerned with them at three stages of their lives. First when, after leaving the egg, under water, they are nymphs. Trout feed on them more at this stage than at any other. With the majority of flies in the family, the nymph or underwater stage of life lasts a year, but

there are those with whom it is two years and may even be three.

At the end of the nymphal stage they rise to the surface of the water and split open along the back, and from the shuck of their old selves emerges the new. This is the first part of their lives as a fly, and at this stage they are known to fishermen as duns. They now have the typical form of the family, upstanding wings, upcurved body, and two or three tails, according to species. The general colouring is dull and the wings semi-opaque. They float on the surface for a brief time waiting for their wings to dry. Many are taken by the trout at this stage, and by other fish too.

PETER GETS OUT LINE AGAIN AND DROPS HIS FLY SOFTLY JUST ABOVE THE TROUT. —HE WAITS IN ACUTE SUSPENSE AS IT FLOATS DOWN

HE'S TAKEN IT! AND THIS TIME YOU WEREN'T TOO QUICK WITH YOUR STRIKE

DROP YOUR ROD SIDEWAYS! THEN IT WON'T FALL ON THE GUT AND SMASH IT

DRAW IT OVER THE NET— IT'S PLAYED OUT NOW

WELL, THERE YOU ARE, PETER— YOUR FIRST TROUT!

A FLY IS DRAGGING WHEN IT SKATES ON THE SURFACE INSTEAD OF FLOATING NATURALLY

SLOWER CURRENT

FAST CURRENT

THERE'S A FISH RISING, PETER, BUT YOU'LL HAVE TO LOOK OUT FOR DRAG. NO TROUT WILL TAKE A DRAGGING FLY!

YOU MUST CAST A LOOSE LINE. AS THE LINE FLIES FORWARD, PULL THE ROD BACK A BIT AND THEN FORWARD AGAIN— THAT'S RIGHT

NOW THE FLY WON'T DRAG UNTIL IT'S PASSED OVER THE FISH

THE FISH HASN'T TAKEN IT!— RECOVER YOUR FLY AND TRY AGAIN. DON'T SNATCH IT OFF!— DRAW SMOOTHLY WITH THE ROD AND DRAW IN LINE WITH YOUR LEFT HAND— YOU CAN SHOOT IT WHEN YOU CAST AGAIN

THAT'S RIGHT— NOW WILL THE FISH RISE THIS TIME?

But presently those that survive flutter rather heavily from the water, and find a resting place on a post or the underside of a leaf.

There they remain for a few hours if the weather is warm, though it may be much longer in colder weather, even a few days. Then they split along the back again, and now emerges the final stage, a perfect little fly. The wings, formerly dull, are now brilliant and glassy, transparent and glancing with iridescent colour. The whole insect is now as brilliant and delicate as it was formerly dull. Some of the males have outstanding eyes of bright orange or russet red. In this stage again its life is brief, often a mere few hours. To the fisherman it is now a spinner. Soon mating takes place, and then the female flies back to the river to lay her eggs. This done she falls exhausted on the surface with wings outspread and dies. She is now the fisherman's spent spinner. At this stage too the flies are taken greedily by the trout.

The principal members of the family are these. First, when the season opens is the Blue Dun or Large Spring Olive. About the same time or very soon after come the Olive Dun, the Iron Blue, and the March Brown. This latter is more a fly of the rocky rivers and is not seen on the chalk streams.

Then about May comes the Pale Watery Dun, followed in late May or early June by the biggest member of the family, the Mayfly. The female is an inch in length and makes a fine meal to which the trout respond furiously. Big trout that at no other time bother about flies will now rise and feast with the rest. In June comes the blue Winged Olive, and this again is a fly that will set every fish in the river feeding with enthusiasm. It is almost entirely a fly of the evening, and many a fisherman tries frantically to find the right artificial fly for it before the light goes, for it is a difficult fly to imitate. Those then are the chief members of the family, though the fisherman of the chalk streams gets to know others which sometimes concern him.

In addition to the *Ephemeridæ* there is the Alder which comes in May and is a great favourite. From May onwards the sedge flies are of importance as flies of the late afternoon and evening, till just as the light is going a really big trout may be taken on the Great Red Sedge.

On the rocky rivers of the north and west the Stonefly is to anglers what the Mayfly is elsewhere.

Besides those I have mentioned there is an assortment of other flies which the fisherman will come to know with experience.

These are the flies that Mr. Crabtree uses

| Blue Dun | Olive Dun | Greenwell's Glory | Gold-ribbed Hare's Ear | Iron Blue Dun | Ginger Quill | Orange Quill | Red Quill |

The Blue Dun is an imitation of the earliest natural fly of the fisherman's season. The Olive Dun is an imitation of the natural fly of that name and can be used all through the season. Greenwell's Glory is one of the best suggestions of several of the Ephemeridæ ever invented. It is good all through the season. Gold-ribbed Hare's Ear also suggests several natural flies and is an all-round-the-season fly. The Iron Blue Dun imitates the natural fly of that name, and when the fish are taking it, it is a deadly fly. The Ginger Quill is a general fly which particularly suggests the Pale Watery Dun. The Orange Quill is a very valuable fly when trout are feeding on the Blue Winged Olive. The Red Quill is a good general fly which will take trout that are feeding on olives. It is known as the 'Dry fly man's sheet anchor on a strange river.'

| Olive Horse Hair | Blue Horse Hair | Red tag | Wickham's Fancy | Caperer | Grannom | Silver Sedge | Medium Sedge |

Here are two flies which Mr. Crabtree tied himself. The first one has a body of white horsehair over a hook shank painted a strong olive colour which shows through the horse hair. The second one has the horse hair over a blue shank. He has found both very successful. The Red Tag is a good fancy fly, particularly for grayling. Wickham's Fancy is another very fancy fly that is sometimes deadly. This pattern called the Caperer was invented by the Late W. F. Lunn and is a very good fly indeed under many different conditions. The Grannom is an imitation of the natural sedge fly of that name that comes in April, and is the earliest of the sedges. The rest of the sedge flies appear from May onwards. There are many of them, but two or three artificial patterns will imitate most of them. Here are two reliable patterns to use through the season.

| Coch-y-bondhu | Soldier Palmer | Mr. Crabtree's Mayfly | Mayfly | Mr. Crabtree's Mayfly Spinner (spent gnat) | March Brown | Tup's Indispensable | Alder |

The Coch-y-bondhu imitates a beetle but it is a good general fly to use at all times. The Soldier Palmer is a fancy fly that will often take trout on rocky rivers. It is also a very good fly for chub if used in a large size, say 3 or 4 or even larger. There is no end to the patterns of the Mayfly. Those shown are good. The first one is one tied by Mr. Crabtree. In general the hackle patterns are very much better than those with wings. This is also the case with other flies, though not so much as with mayflies. The March Brown imitates the natural fly of the same name, and is good all round the season on rocky streams. Tup's Indispensable is an excellent general fly which imitates several spinners. The Alder is a very good fly when the natural Alder is on the water, but it will also take fish at many other times, even when the Mayfly is on.

SUMMER

NOW here are the halcyon days of the fisherman. This is the lovely period when for many fishermen it is the return to the river and the lake. Unless he is a fly fisherman he will have spent three months in exile waiting for this moment. And in many seasons this return has all the setting that it should have. How many seasons I can remember when the 16th June has come with a spell of warm and settled weather. Early June may have been cold, overcast, anything but what it should be. But by the 16th a change has come, and the fisherman's first day has dawned still, clear and warm, the way it does in the hot weather of early summer.

So five o'clock will find the angler at the waterside, putting up his rod beside the swim that he has so carefully baited up in advance of this moment. For it is more than probable he is going to fish for tench, and that is an early morning game to have the best of it. The tench is so much a fish of high summer. No other is quite so suitable for this first morning. The carp too is very much a summer fish; just as much a fish of early morning lakes with hardly a breath to stir them. But the carp is a very uncertain fish. You may have to wait many hours before that sudden hurricane comes that means that you have hooked a carp. On other mornings, mornings subsequent to this first one, we are ready to wait these hours, fruitless though they often are in the outcome. But this morning it is proper that we should catch some fish. It is part of the delicious, idle perfection of the occasion. For to me, though there comes all the action of hooking and playing, there is a trance-like idling about it all.

and the fisherman

The morning has such a fragile loveliness that it seems far removed from ordinary reality.

If the water is of any quality, and the baiting has been well done in advance, it may reasonably be relied upon that the tench will play their part. Those slow oily bubbles will drift to the surface, hang there lazily, and burst. You know that tench are about.

But should you have to wait for this, or should there be long pauses between the fish that take your bait, time will not weigh upon you. Your sense of the hours will be numbed. You will not have a thought beyond your fishing and the things about you.

However much immersed in his fishing the angler is, he cannot be indifferent to the activities of the many creatures round him. He has the amplest opportunity to see them, for he is such a still figure that he is not heeded by the lake's inhabitants. They come and go, regarding him no more than if he were a stump. He sees the mallard duck shepherding her half-grown family on intent but apparently aimless journeyings over the water, folding the glassy surface into oily crinkles. The kingfisher drops from its bough over the water, exploding it into momentary fragments. Then it reappears, a tiny fish gripped in its beak.

The heron lifts heavily from the shallows, its trailing legs seeming hard to carry. The swans preen and arch, and inspect the fisherman with an arrogant stare, leaving him unmolested only because he is so still. Sudden little clusters of fry break from the surface in a terrified flurry. A perch is feeding.

Tench

The fishes of Summer

THESE are the fishes of summer, each in its way beloved of the fisherman. Each has its own special associations deeply significant to those that have fished for it. For each there is a band of adherents specially devoted to its pursuit. There is not one of them which has not its followers for whom it is an obsession. But for many of us, less single-minded, these are all fine fish to angle for.

The tench, as I have said, is for many the symbol of the new season. It is, perhaps, more than any other the totem fish of summer. How many early mornings, how many translucent twilights we can remember when the tench have set the reeds swaying, and finally our floats have wavered, dipped and dithered, and then slid away. The fat and gleaming fish have slid into the net, brown, shot with green, with a golden patina over all, wonderfully set off by the little crimson eye.

Then the bream, the stately sailing bream, that is almost an insignia for the anglers of East Anglia. What a tradition of fine summer sport is associated with its name! What nights and mornings of sport old bream fishers can recall! The great days of breaming perhaps are gone.

Bream

Carp

It may be that they were too lavishly indulged in for the good of the species. Too many catches measured by the stone were carried dead from the water. The greater enlightenment that has come to fishermen has come too late to stop much damage being done. Then the disastrous sea flood that inundated so much of the Norfolk Broads in 1938 killed off vast numbers. Broadsmen say that bream are still not seen in the great shoals that used to be. But time will improve this.

If the evil of pollution can be eradicated, and proper fish conservation carried out on a national scale, bream and all other fish will increase and flourish.

Of all the fish of summer the carp is unrivalled. No other can give such sport. But not all fisherman are equal to the test of it. For he who fishes for carp must be ready to do so with the greatest devotion. He must be ready to wait long hours of tense inactivity, that often in the end culminate in nothing. But when a climax does come to the vigil, it may be so tempestuous that many a fisherman is not equal to it. The carp is a fish scornful of coarse tackle but powerful enough to break the strongest.

The barbel is a fish of the gravelly deeps. It lies in the clear chasms of water strongly scoured by the current. It is much sought in weir pools and such places. And as might be expected from this, it is a strong fish that disputes hard for its liberty. Nowhere is it found in such size and perfection as on the Hampshire Avon at Christchurch.

Barbel

The River in Summer

THE river as we find it now is very different from its state as we have already seen it in winter. The sharp clear outlines of it are softened and obscured. The geography of the water is more subtly complicated. In winter the division between main current and quiet water was sharply defined, and therefore easy to interpret. Now the component parts of the river are less easily seen one from another.

All this change has meant a change in the life of the fish population. It is more widely distributed over the river. There is no longer any part which is more or less untenable as there was in winter. Chub, for instance, that in winter had retired almost entirely to the deep eddies, may now be met almost anywhere, particularly early in the season. Still, however, they keep their preference for tree-shaded swims. Perch, that by autumn will be in the deep holes, are now much more widely scattered, even in the clear runs between the weed beds (WB). Generally, at this time of the year the proximity of weed means fish.

A – marks swims that will certainly hold chub. They may hold other fish too – roach, dace, perch; but chub may be depended on. B – too, though having a mixed population, will be sure to have chub: a tree shaded eddy is always a happy home for chub. C – marks those little eddies behind bridge piers and weed beds where many fish may wait for what the stream brings them. Such eddies can also be found behind shoulders of bank. D – marks the sort of shallow run that may be found under the bank, and is often a place for gudgeon and minnows for bait.

53

Mr Crabtree and Peter open the season with tench,
a typical summer fish.

I HAVE emphasized already how much tench fishing is associated in my mind with the opening of the coarse fishing season. Perhaps I have over-emphasized it. There may be many anglers for whom the 16th of June means more particularly some other fish.

But there is no doubt that these early days of the season are the golden time for tench. And there could be no more delightful way of opening the season than this. Those perfect, pearly mornings and serene, slowly sinking evenings are the very essence that justifies for fishing the title of 'the contemplative man's recreation.' In them is the perfect blend of utter peace and excitement.

Tench fishing is above all a business of the early morning and the evening after the sun has left the water. And for the best chance it must be warm, still weather. A chill in the air, or a wind crisping the water, and the fishing is seldom as good. As with everything in fishing, there is no finality about this. Days may be had when the tench will not cease to feed all day. Sometimes the most unpromising conditions of lowering skies and cool winds will produce sport. But these are exceptions. Generally, fine, still weather is needed. Sport will usually be over by 8.30 a.m. and will not restart until the coming of evening. Then it may continue until it is too dark to see a float.

THERE ARE NO BAD SNAGS HERE SO WE'RE USING 3X GUT. YOU'RE GOING TO USE FLOAT TACKLE AND I'M USING FLOAT LEDGER

MY FLOAT IS A LONG ONE ATTACHED BY THE BOTTOM RING ONLY — A VERY SENSITIVE METHOD. I'M USING A LOBWORM AS BAIT ON A N° 6 ROUND-BEND HOOK

TO ROD TOP →

SPLIT SHOT TO STOP LEDGER BULLET

PIERCED BULLET FREE TO RUN UP AND DOWN GUT

YOU'RE USING A SMALL FLOAT WITH ABOUT 10 INCHES OF GUT LYING ON THE BOTTOM. YOUR BAIT IS A LARGE KNOB OF PASTE ON A N° 6 HOOK

TO MAKE PASTE SOAK BREAD AND SQUEEZE AND KNEED IN HAND OR CLEAN CLOTH UNTIL IT IS STIFF PASTE

WE'LL SEE WHICH IS MORE ATTRACTIVE TO THE TENCH THIS MORNING — SOMETIMES IT'S ONE, SOMETIMES THE OTHER

FOR TWENTY MINUTES NOTHING HAPPENS — THEN...

BUBBLES COME SLOWLY TO THE SURFACE

LOOK AT YOUR FLOAT, PETER, DON'T TOUCH IT YET — WAIT!

PETER'S FLOAT STARTS TO DITHER

THE FLOAT BECOMES STILL, THEN DITHERS AGAIN — THEN...

LOOK, DAD, IT'S LYING FLAT!

YES, PETER, WAIT!

PRESENTLY IT MOVES ACROSS THE WATER AND SLIDES UNDER

NOW, PETER — STRIKE!

I SAY, DAD, IT CAN PULL! IT'S RUN TEN YARDS AND NOT STOPPED YET!

This early and late habit of the tench is only one of the things about it unfavourable to the casual angler who must get to the water as and when he can; for the chances of success are greatly increased if previous baiting of the swim is done. If for several days in advance of fishing groundbait is put into the swim, sport can almost be relied upon if conditions are right otherwise. I do not wish to suggest that tench cannot be caught without this, but it is very much more of a gamble. To catch tench consistently you fish early and late, and ground-bait in advance.

As might be expected with a fish of such quiet and peaceful associations, there is nothing sudden about the bite of a tench.

Indeed, it is quite the most leisurely biting of all fishes, unless we except the prolonged fiddling of an eel. The angler is given ample time to prepare himself for the vital moment. The first indication is often a slight lifting and leaning of the float that has previously been as still as if painted on the water. This is electrifying enough to the fisherman. Then it may begin to roll a little or move slowly across the surface. Or it may become quite still again, and remain so for several minutes. This sort of thing may be brief, but it can go on for minutes together. But sooner or later the float will develop a more certain movement and then slide away and under. That is the moment for the angler.

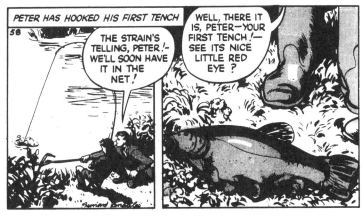

Now he may strike and not, I hope, with the violence with which I have sometimes seen it done. From this point on the tench fully makes amends for its previous slowness, for it is a fine fighter whose first run is long enough to surprise anyone who has not fished for it before. Then afterwards it is a very satisfying start to the season to see this fat and lovely fish upon the bank.

Opinion is often divided as to the best way to fish, float or ledger. Most fishermen will, I think, come down on the side of float, if for no other reason than that it is so good once more to see a float and wait for its message. But as Mr. Crabtree shows, the best method may often be something of both, the float

ledger. In any place where it can be used, this is an excellent method. It is very sensitive and less influenced by any breeze if there should be one. For boat fishing, float fishing is certainly better. The slight roll and drift of the boat at its mooring pulls at the ledger and agitates the float.

There is no finality about baits for tench. It may be said that bread paste is the best all-round bait, but there are many occasions when other baits will do better. Sometimes it will be worm, a big lobworm. But there are times when tench are finicky and nothing but a little red worm will take them. Other times again it must be nothing but a bunch of gentles.

NOW, PETER, FOR CARP—— THE KING OF THE SUMMER. THE FISH THAT MAKES YOU WAIT LONGEST BUT GIVES YOU THE MADDEST THRILL!

THE carp fisherman is frequently a specialist. Any angler can fish for carp from time to time, and from time to time he may have successes. He may catch those middle-sized carp up to about ten pounds. But the epic captures are most often made by men for whom carp are an obsession, a life study.

For large carp are not ordinary fish. The casual approach of the angler seeking a change from roach or perch will seldom take them. They have what may easily be taken for enormous wisdom. There is something about them which seems almost uncanny, so fine is their sense of what is safe for them.

And supposing the angler does overcome their suspicions and get as far as hooking them. Even then his chances of landing his quarry are often slight. The carp fights as no other fish can fight. His power is enormous. A middle-sized fish, no more than 8 to 10 pounds, goes off with a rush too heavy to stop. To try to stop it means the certainty of loss. The eternal problem with carp is to use tackle fine enough to deceive the fish and yet strong enough to give any chance of landing it.

UP WITH THE LARK AGAIN, PETER. TO CATCH CARP YOU FISH EARLY OR FISH LATE. BUT IT'S WORTH IT.— THE CARP IS THE GREATEST FIGHTER OF THEM ALL!

I'VE BEEN BAITING THE SWIM FOR SEVERAL DAYS WITH WASTE STALE BREAD MIXED WITH SAND AND LITTLE PAR-BOILED POTATOES

SEE I'VE MARKED THE PLACE WITH A REED ANCHORED BY A STONE

WELL, NOW WE'VE TACKLED UP, AN 11 FT. ROD, WHOLE CANE BUTT, SPLIT CANE MIDDLE AND TOP JOINTS, NO FLOAT, NO LEAD, A 1½ YD. 1 X CAST

FOR BAIT WE'LL USE A PAR-BOILED POTATO ABOUT THE SIZE OF A BLACK-BIRD'S EGG, COOKED IN ITS SKIN, BUT SKINNED BEFORE USE

WITH A BAITING NEEDLE I THREAD THROUGH IT A TREBLE HOOK-TO-GUT. I HIDE THE HOOK IN THE BAIT—FOR THIS YOUR HANDS *MUST* BE CLEAN, THE BAIT MUSTN'T BE TAINTED.

I have heard one successful carp fisherman say that the only proper compromise is fine 'Elasticum' wire, and I think there may be a lot to be said for this. It would be difficult to find gut that could match it for the combination of all the qualities needed, fineness, strength, and lack of visibility.

You see, the very great strength of carp is problem enough, but frequently they are found in water which has an abundance of weed. Often this includes lily pads, and once you let your carp get into that and it is not very probable that you will see him again. Fine wire would give you a better chance than gut.

Carping demands a great capacity for waiting, and it is this which so often induces the ignorant to talk of the patience of fishermen. But the truth is that it is not patience at all that holds the carp fisherman to his vigil. It is an intensity of suspense. Carp fishing is one of the most acutely exciting of all forms of fishing. In the system of the confirmed carp fisher it works like a drug. He becomes like a man apart.

Probably the best method in the long run of taking big carp is ledgering in a swim that has been previously baited for several days. Over a period this will yield more big carp than any other way. And equally the best long-term hook baits are a large lump of paste or a small potato that has been boiled to the point

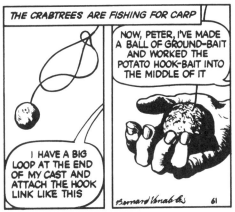

THE CRABTREES ARE FISHING FOR CARP

NOW, PETER, I'VE MADE A BALL OF GROUND-BAIT AND WORKED THE POTATO HOOK-BAIT INTO THE MIDDLE OF IT

I HAVE A BIG LOOP AT THE END OF MY CAST AND ATTACH THE HOOK LINK LIKE THIS

WHEN I PUT THAT REED AS A MARKER OF THE GROUND-BAIT I MEASURED OFF JUST HOW MUCH LINE IT TOOK TO REACH IT AND TIED A PIECE OF COTTON ON THE LINE. WE'LL PULL OFF LINE UP TO THE COTTON AND CAST FROM THE COIL

AS MR CRABTREE PULLS OFF THE LINE, HE COILS IT ON A PIECE OF BROWN PAPER

NOW I PUT THE ROD IN A REST AND REVERSE THE COILS SO THAT THEY GO OUT THE RIGHT WAY

NOW OUT GOES THE TACKLE WITH AN UNDERHAND SWING

I REEL UP THE LOOSE LINE AND PULL OFF A FEW FEET FROM THE REEL AND COIL IT ON THE GROUND

NOW WHILE WE WAIT THE GROUND-BAIT IS SOFTENING AWAY FROM THE HOOK-BAIT AND THE CARP—WE HOPE—ARE TRYING IT —

UNTIL THEY COME TO THE POTATO ON THE HOOK

TIME PASSES

THEY HAVE BECOME USED TO FINDING LITTLE POTATOES IN THE GROUND-BAIT

HALF-AN-HOUR GOES BY

THE LOOSE LINE'S GOING!

when it is still firm and fairly hard - parboiled as they say. But this is by no means the end of either methods or baits. For the middle-sized fish, with which we all-round fishermen are concerned, there is a variety of ways.

But in all these techniques there is one common factor. They are all based on the great cunning of carp.

The most obvious way is the ordinary float-fishing with the bait and eighteen inches of gut lying on the bottom. The bait may be the two I have mentioned or others. Honey mixed into the paste is said to be very compelling to carp. It may be so. Paste made from bread and potatoes is another. Lobworms, gentles, and wasp grubs may all take carp on their days.

On warm days carp will often lie near the surface, sunning themselves, and then a cast made so that the gut lies across the lily leaves with bait hanging a little way below will sometimes bring results. If there is a wind the gut may be attached to a lily leaf and allowed to sail out before the wind until it is over the fish.

Another method for a windy day is to insert the hook, not smaller than size 6, in a fairly large piece of bread, and allow that to drift out before the wind. Carp will come up to take it.

Whatever method is used, all baits must be absolutely clean. No taint must be on them. With your parboiled potato, leave it in its skin until you put it on the hook. Then peel it with clean fingers and thread the gut of the hook through it with a baiting needle.

LET'S SEE IF WE CAN CATCH THE STATELY BREAM, PETER, THERE'S GOOD SPORT TO BE HAD IF YOU CAN FIND A SHOAL. THEY'RE NOT GREAT FIGHTERS, BUT IT'S A PLEASANT GAME FOR ALL THAT!

THE Crabtrees, as you see, are coming to the river in the evening for their bream fishing. And the later they stay by the river, the better is their fishing likely to be. Conversely, had they come instead in the early morning, the later they stayed the less good was it likely to be. Some success with bream fishing may be had at most times of the day, but unquestionably morning and evening are best. It is then and through the night that bream feed most consistently.

In former days it was the custom in the great bream districts of East Anglia to fish all night, and then quite immense catches were made. These catches were, in fact, too immense, for it was not the way of these fishermen to return their catches alive. Now, fortunately, constantly more anglers realise that if fishing is to continue, stock must be conserved.

But then there was no such inhibition, and all fish caught were taken away. A fisherman has to work harder for his bream now and is the better for it.

AS THE SUN IS GOING DOWN THE CRABTREES COME TO THE RIVER BANK

THIS IS A LIKELY BREAM HOLE, PETER, DEEP AND QUIET AWAY FROM THE HEAVY WATER

EARLY MORNING OR EVENING IS BEST, THOUGH YOU CAN CATCH BREAM DURING THE DAY

AND LOOK—THERE **ARE** BREAM ABOUT— WE'RE NONE TOO SOON. THEY'VE STARTED TO FEED — SEE THE MUDDIED WATER AND THE BUBBLES RISING!

I'LL THROW IN SOME GROUND-BAIT BEFORE WE TACKLE UP. GOOD GROUND-BAIT IS BREAD, BRAN AND BOILED POTATO—

BUT WE MUST MANAGE WITH STALE BREAD SCRAPS, SAND, AND BOILED POTATO PEELINGS

WE'LL USE OUR 11 FT. RODS AGAIN, WITH 3X CASTS AND Nº7 HOOK-TO-GUT, AND A SMALL FLOAT TO CARRY 3 OR 4 SHOT

65

WE'LL USE BREAD PASTE FOR BAIT—A LARGE ROUGH KNOB OF IT THAT COVERS THE HOOK. YOU MUST HAVE CLEAN HANDS SO THAT THE BAIT ISN'T TAINTED!

NOW WE'VE FOUND THE DEPTH, SO WE'LL SET OUR FLOATS SO THAT THE LAST 12" OF GUT LIE ON THE BOTTOM

NOW WE'VE GOT OUR TACKLE OUT WHERE THE GROUND-BAIT IS, WE'LL PUT RODS IN REST AND WAIT

THE CRABTREES ARE LUCKY—THEY HAVE FOUND THE BREAM FEEDING

PRESENTLY MR CRABTREE'S FLOAT RISES AND WAVES GENTLY

MR CRABTREE'S FLOAT IN THE BREAM SWIM RISES AND LIES FLAT

WAIT!

NOW STRIKE!

THE FISH IS HOOKED AND BORES DEEP

I MUST STEER IT AWAY FROM THE REST OF THE SHOAL

THAT'S IT, PETER—GET THE NET UNDER HIM!

East Anglia is still the kingdom of the bream. In Suffolk, Norfolk, Lincolnshire, and the Fens bream are everywhere. In the still-water fisheries of this area it is the custom to look for patches of muddied water that tell that bream are present, rooting on the bottom for their food. But they tell me on the Broads that this is much less so than formerly. It may be that the numbers of bream are not so great as they were. But certainly they must be looked for more closely. This at least is the case of those Broads that were affected by the sea flood, such as Horsey Mere and Hickling. There seems no reason why in time the bream shoals should not be as great as ever.

But when such a muddied piece of water is found, the method in Norfolk is to moor the boat very quietly within long casting range. Ground bait is thrown in and the baited tackle follows. When a fish is hooked it is drawn away from the rest of the shoal as soon as possible to avoid disturbing them.

River fishing is rather less simple. Mr. Crabtree's fishing as seen here is quite typical of much river fishing for bream. There are many rivers in various parts of the country where conditions are like this. But the swim will not necessarily be under the bank as it is here. There is a type of swim, common for instance on the Great Ouse, which is a hole or declivity in the river bed in the main course of the river. Such a hole may often be detected by the absence of weed in an otherwise weedy stretch. If the river

is not too wide it can be fished from the bank with a ledger or float ledger tackle cast out rather downstream so that it straightens out from rod top to bait.

But often the river is too wide. Then a boat must be used. It should be moored well above the swim, and the tackle, preferably ledger, cast down into the swim.

On many of these bream rivers some of the best fishing is in the lower reaches where the stream runs strong and deep. Here the only possible method is ledgering, and it may have to be really heavy ledgering. Where the tide races, only a heavy lead will hold the bottom.

It need not be supposed that all this fishing is early morning or evening. It is simply that the best fishing is to be had

then. Sport, if of a less reliable kind, can be had during the day too.

Probably the best all-round bait for bream is paste. Lobworms are often excellent, but with these the nuisance of eels is often enough to drive the angler back on to paste. Other baits are gentles, wasp grubs, and stewed wheat. Whatever is used should be used generously. Bream like a good mouthful. And as with carp, it must be clean. The least suggestion of tobacco is quite fatal.

In all this I have been talking of the bronze or common bream. There is another in many waters in East Anglia and in some other places, the white or silver bream. This is small, greedy, and, where it abounds, an unmitigated nuisance. It cannot be kept from taking the bait meant for better fish.

BAITS *how to prepare them and preserve them*

TO talk of baits for fishing inevitably starts with worms. There are various types of worm, but the fisherman is mainly concerned with three. First is the lobworm, the large one common in any garden. It is a good bait for tench, carp, chub, perch, barbel and bream. The tail of it is a first-rate bait for roach in coloured water and often for several other fish.

The red worm is the little bright one with iridescence on it that is found in rotting leaves and under old damp sacking. Another small worm is the brandling which is found in old manure heaps.

All worms should be treated before use to toughen and brighten them. This is done by keeping them for a few days in a vessel which contains damp moss. The worms should be put on top of the moss and left. They will soon work down through it to the bottom. Each day the moss should be inverted so that the worms will work through again. Dead ones must be taken out.

Second to worms in the wideness of its application is paste. It is best made by taking the inside of a loaf, soaking it and kneading it in a cloth until it takes on the close and adhesive consistency of paste. Variants can be made by working in honey (for carp) or cheese (for chub and barbel). Paste can also be made from flour and water. Cheese alone is good chub bait.

The next important bait is gentles, which are no more than the larval form of the common bluebottle. This again comes near to being a universal bait. They can be bought ready scoured from tackle shops, in meal or bran. If they are not to be used the same day they should be kept in a dark cool place, or they will quickly become chrysalids.

A first-rate bait for various fish, is bread crust. This may be prepared by cutting off the outside of a stale loaf so that it is half crust and half crumb. Put a damp cloth over it and leave it under a weight. Before use it can be cut into squares. Another way is to soak the whole loaf and then cut off the crust in the same way as before, and finally cut into squares. It can be given a less artificial appearance by tearing off pieces as required. Cubes of the inside of a loaf make a very good bait.

Both breadcrust and the inside of the loaf can be used unsoaked as a floating bait.

An unsurpassed summer bait for roach that will also take other fish is silk weed. This is the weed that clothes the sills of weirs and such places. It should not be touched by hand. The hook should be passed through the weed as it grows and brought away with the weed festooning it. Use it in the places where the fish may expect it to come to them, weir pools for example.

Elderberries in their season will take roach and chub, and for chub various other fruits can be used.

Stewed wheat is a bait that at times is unrivalled for roach and other bottom-feeding fish. It should be boiled slowly in water till, having swelled to several times its original size, the outer skin splits. Pearl barley can also be boiled slowly to make a good bait. Hempseed is a deadly bait that has gained an undeserved reputation of being bad for fish. It should be stewed very slowly until small white cracks appear.

Almost any small fish will make a good live bait, and preserved they are good for spinning. Small roach, dace, gudgeon, minnows, loaches and bleak can all be used. Mr. Alexander Wanless gives a very good way of preserving them. The baits should be killed by putting them in a solution of a tablespoonful of formalin in a pint of water. Leave them in this for about a couple of days. Then wash them in cold water and put them in a shallow dish containing a syrup of one part of sugar to four of water. After a few days, during which the taint of formalin will go, bottle them in another mixing of the same syrup.

Nowadays sugar is not to be had for such a purpose. So after washing them, bottle them in a very much weaker solution of the formalin. I have caught many fish on baits not wholly rid of their formalin flavour.

AUTUMN
the golden season

FOR all-round results, autumn is probably the best season for the coarse fisherman. All fish are still to be caught and have come into condition. And they are mostly settled in their typical quarters. In those deep eddies under the bank (E), chub and perch will have congregated. The distribution of fish otherwise will depend on the nature of the season. If it is still summery, roach and dace will be more or less all over the river. Chub may be met with in the easy streams, and even perch. But if it is an early autumn with strong water and lower temperatures, the roach and dace will be out of the strongest water, and the chub and perch will have retired to the quiet deeps. Bream will be in quiet deep water. Barbel will be in deep holes over the gravel but out of the main force. Pike will be under the tree roots, in the mouths of side-streams (SS), and lurking at the edge of the easy currents.

> SEPTEMBER – OCTOBER IS A VERY GOOD TIME FOR BARBEL — PARTICULARLY IF THE WEATHER IS WARM. AND WHAT SPORT IT IS! THE BARBEL IS A POWERFUL FISH!

FISHING for barbel is not what it was. It is not the quality which has changed. Superb barbel fishing is still to be had in places.

No, it is the method that has changed. In more spacious days when some people at least had more money, barbel fishing was undertaken on the most expansive scale. A strict ritual was followed. First a vast supply of worms was bought. And the number used, many thousands, must even then have been a great expense. Into the selected swim these were dumped, a huge mass of them, every morning for several days in advance of that chosen for the operation. If you were one of the really princely coarse-fishermen in which the period seemed to abound, you had a man to do this for you. He received the worms and deposited them in the swim. Your investment was made and the place of deposit marked with a ryepeck. That was the proper instrument. Then on the appointed day you arrived, unsullied by worm until this moment. Perhaps you remained so.

THE CRABTREES ARE GOING BARBEL FISHING

THE OLD WAY OF BARBEL FISHING, PETER, WAS TO BAIT UP FOR SEVERAL DAYS BEFORE FISHING WITH THOUSANDS OF WORMS, BUT YOU CAN CATCH BARBEL WITHOUT ALL THAT BOTHER — AND EXPENSE

70

WE'LL DO IT THE WAY THEY DO ON THE HAMPSHIRE AVON — AND THEY GET MAGNIFICENT BARBEL THERE

OUR 11 FT. ROD IS THE BEST. WHOLE CANE BOTTOM JOINT, MIDDLE AND TOP JOINTS SPLIT CANE

WE'LL USE A BIG FLOAT TO CARRY PLENTY OF SHOT TO GET DOWN TO THE FISH IN THE STRONG WATER. THE CAST IS 2X, AND THE HOOK Nº 9 ON 3X GUT

HERE'S OUR SWIM, THE WATER COMES DOWN FAST AND SHALLOW, THEN SPREADS INTO DEEPER WATER OVER A GRAVEL BOTTOM. ALWAYS LOOK FOR GRAVEL IF YOU WANT BARBEL

DEEPER WATER

SHALLOW RUN

NOW WE MUST PUT IN SOME GROUND-BAIT!— THE PROPER WAY TO MAKE IT IS TO MIX STALE BREAD, BRAN AND SOME SORT OF MEAL. BUT WE MUST MAKE DO WITH WASTE BREAD SCRAPS, A BAG OF CLOUD GROUND-BAIT AND SOME CLAY TO SINK IT—WE'LL MIX IN SOME GENTLES AS WE'RE GOING TO USE THEM ON THE HOOK

I'LL THROW IT IN WELL UPSTREAM OF THE SWIM — THEN IT WILL REACH BOTTOM IN THE SWIM

THERE'S ABOUT 7FT. OF WATER IN THE SWIM, SO I'LL SET THE FLOAT AT 8FT. THEN THE BAIT WILL DRAG BOTTOM

WE'LL HAVE A BUNCH OF GENTLES FOR BAIT— LIKE THIS

I CHECK THE FLOAT A LITTLE TO GET IT OVER THE SHALLOW WATER

IN THE SWIM I LET THE TACKLE FLOAT NATURALLY AT THE PACE OF THE STREAM. THE BAIT IS TRIPPING AND DRAGGING BOTTOM

THE CRABTREES ARE AFTER BARBEL

AT THE END OF THE SWIM I HOLD IT A MOMENT SO THAT THE BAIT WAVERS INVITINGLY IN THE PLAY OF THE CURRENT

FOR SOME TIME NOTHING HAPPENS — THE CRABTREES FISH ON —

BUT BENEATH THE SURFACE—

Perhaps your man put the lobworm on the hook and dropped in the further mass of worms that started the fishing.

Then according to the proper order of things great sport was enjoyed. Quite often results did equal expectation, but there were many other occasions when the total reward for all the outlay of money and your man's effort was one roach.

The method used in this fishing was ledgering, generally with a good large lead, for barbel tend to lie where the deep water scours hard over the gravel. Weir pools were a favourite place, particularly on the Thames. But this is by no means the only sort of place where barbel are to be found. Early in the season they may be in quite shallow water. All through the season clear lively water of fair depth over a gravel bottom may hold them. I remember a piece of water on the Kennet where the current ran fast with a depth of about five or six feet. This water was about 100 yards below a mill, and great trusses of weed swayed in the current. In the unseen channels through the weed lay many barbel, and the loud sucking noises they made could be heard from far off. They were one of the many glories of this reach of the Kennet, a beautiful reach. Now all that is done. The bed has been dredged, the alternation of lovely shallows and deep seductive pools has been swept away.

AT THE SURFACE THE FLOAT GOES UNDER BOLDLY, DECIDEDLY

A FIRM STRIKE— AND IT'S ON!

THE BARBEL GOES OFF WITH A HEAVY RUSH, BORING DEEP

CAN YOU HOLD HIM, DAD? HE'LL SMASH THE GUT!

NOT IF I CAN HELP IT!— I'M LETTING THE ROD TOP TAKE THE STRAIN— THAT'S WHAT IT'S FOR!

HE WON'T SMASH THE GUT IF HE DOESN'T FIND A SNAG— THE ROD TOP IS A SHOCK ABSORBER

THE BARBEL FIGHTS LONG AND HARD— BUT AT LAST—

NOW CAREFUL WITH THE NET, PETER—THE LEAST BUNGLE AND WE'LL LOSE HIM YET!

LOOK AT HIM WELL BEFORE WE PUT HIM BACK, PETER— SEE THE TWO BARBELS ON EACH SIDE OF HIS MOUTH?— THAT'S HOW YOU CAN TELL A YOUNG BARBEL FROM A GUDGEON— THE GUDGEON HAS ONLY ONE EACH SIDE!

BARBELS

The river has been canalised, the bends straightened. The matter dredged from the bed has been piled along the banks. The willows that leaned so beautifully over the water have been cut down. The river has been "improved."

I do not know if anyone still fishes in the grand manner for barbel. Certainly most of us do not. Results on good barbel waters show that those immense preparations are not essential for the catching of barbel. Methods used today may not produce the great catches that were sometimes made by the old way, but this is no disadvantage. A moderate catch of good fish amply fulfils the desires of any real fisherman.

The method used here by Mr. Crabtree is one that catches many barbel. A more interesting and sensitive method, I think, than the old.

To ledger for barbel there should be a yard of gut below the shot which is the bottom stop or the ledger lead. A lump of ground bait as large as an orange should be squeezed round the lead. It should be of bread and bran and should also contain something of whatever is used as hook bait - generally a lobworm. And it should be mixed really stiff, even adding clay if necessary. The whole tackle is cast with an easy swing into the head of the barbel swim. The groundbait disintegrates slowly down the swim, a constant invitation to take the hook bait.

Baits for barbel are lobworms, paste, gentles, cheese, silk weed, wasp grubs and bread crust.

THERE'S NOTHING PLEASANTER ON A WARM AUTUMN DAY THAN CASTING A DRY FLY FOR CHUB. THE FISH ARE FIT AND FIGHT WELL ON THE FINE TACKLE!

OFTEN in summer and on into the autumn, there come days when the sun pours down all day, there is no merciful shred of cloud, and the water is like heated metal. Bottom fishermen who are then by the river do not have a profitable time. Nothing disturbs their sleeping floats. There might be no fish in the river.

But is there no indication at all of life below the surface? What are those plops that come from time to time? What causes those rings that appear on the surface? They are caused by fish. But they are not fish that will take a bait. They are rising to flies. Nothing else will interest them in this heat. Walk along a high bank overlooking the water where there is a background to conceal you. You will see big slow chub that drift to the surface, suck in a fly and sink back again. You can catch those fish. But not if you stick to bottom fishing.

If, on the other hand, you approach them with a dry fly, you may have really good sport. Your approach must, of course, be made with the greatest respect.

YES, PETER, DRY FLY FISHING IS ABOUT THE MOST SPORTING AND ENJOYABLE WAY OF CATCHING CHUB. AND THEY'LL TAKE A FLY EVEN IN HOT AND GLARING SUN!

A 8 OR 9 FT. FLY ROD DOES VERY WELL—SPLIT CANE IS BEST, BUT GREEN-HEART IS GOOD TOO—AND MUCH CHEAPER. A 3YD. CAST TAPERED TO 3X IS ABOUT RIGHT. THE LINE IS GREASED AND WE'LL OIL THE FLY—WE'RE FISHING DRY FLY

A GOOD BIG BUZZY FLY IS BEST FOR CHUB—A SOLDIER PALMER FOR INSTANCE, OR AN ORANGE PALMER— ON A HOOK NOT SMALLER THAN 3 OR 4, NEW SCALE

75

EDDY CHUB EDDY CHUB CHUB
CHUB CHUB SLOW WATER AT TAIL OF POOL CHUB
FAST WATER AT HEAD OF POOL CHUB
EDDY EDDY CHUB
CHUB CHUB

THERE ARE PLENTY OF CHUB TO BE FOUND IN A POOL LIKE THIS—WE'LL HAVE TO FISH FROM THE BOAT

69

If you give the least hint of your presence there will be no chub. Chub have at all times an exaggerated awareness of human interest in them, and under these conditions they have the best possible chance of seeing you. So give them all the respect, so far as approach is concerned, that you would give to the most sophisticated trout.

Fly-fishing for trout is, as we know, a matter of small flies that must fall like thistledown. This is quite wasted on chub. Chub will take the delicate trout-fly, as every trout fisherman knows, but to set out for chub another way is better. A good large fly should be used. The chub likes a mouthful. He is a fish that hangs about under overhanging trees waiting for the large caterpillars that may fall from them. He likes a large beetle or any big moth that falls on to the surface. He hears these things alight on the surface with a good plop. He has learnt to respond to this. So it can do no harm if your fly, too, falls in this self-advertising way. At least under trees a fly heavily dropped is quite appropriate.

But this does not mean that any rough and careless fishing will do. Drag is as much to be avoided as it is for trout. The exception to this is deliberate drag. The chub takes many insects that skate across the surface, and a well-hackled fly that is pulled across an eddy with short draws will often induce a chub to take.

WE'LL FISH THE EDDIES DOWN THE OTHER SIDE OF THE POOL. I'LL ROW UP THE EDDY THIS SIDE AND THEN CUT ACROSS THE CURRENT AT THE HEAD OF THE POOL

PATH TAKEN BY MR CRABTREE TO AVOID THE FORCE OF THE CURRENT

NOW I'LL LET THE BOAT FLOAT DOWN QUIETLY WITH THE CURRENT. I'LL HOLD IT WHERE YOU WANT TO FISH. IT'S A BETTER WAY THAN ROWING. ROWING MAKES A DISTURBANCE IN THE WATER AND FRIGHTENS THE CHUB !

TRY A CAST IN THAT EDDY UNDER THE TREES—THERE SHOULD BE CHUB THERE

76

AH, YOU'VE THROWN TOO STRAIGHT A LINE. THE CURRENT WILL SNATCH IT AND MAKE THE FLY SKATE ACROSS THE EDDY

SEE WHAT I MEAN ? YOU SHOULD HAVE THROWN A SNAKY LINE—THEN A CHUB MIGHT HAVE TAKEN BEFORE THE FLY STARTED TO DRAG

NOW WE'RE A LITTLE LOWER TRY UNDER THAT WILLOW AT THE EDGE OF THE CURRENT

77

THE FLY DROPS CLOSE IN TO WHERE THE LEAVES HANG OVER THE WATER. A NOSE COMES UP AND THE FLY DISAPPEARS

STRIKE, PETER! — NOT TOO QUICKLY, CHUB ARE SLOW TAKERS!

AH, HE'S SMASHED YOU IN ALL THAT TANGLE — CHUB ALWAYS DIVE FOR THE ROOTS. YOU OUGHT TO HUSTLE THEM OUT QUICKLY. TIE ON ANOTHER FLY

NOW CAST ACROSS THIS BIG EDDY — THERE ARE BOUND TO BE CHUB UNDER THAT BUSH. AS THE EDDY TURNS BACK UPSTREAM HERE YOU NEED TO CAST IN A DOWN-RIVER DIRECTION

PETERS FIRST CAST FALLS ABOUT 18" OUT — NOTHING HAPPENS

78
HE CASTS AGAIN, ONLY A FEW INCHES OUT —

THE FLY DISAPPEARS

NOW STRIKE AND DRAW QUICKLY WITH YOUR LEFT HAND — GET HIM AWAY FROM THE ROOTS!

NOW YOU'VE GOT HIM IN THE OPEN AND YOU HAVE THE BEATING OF HIM!

THERE'S ALWAYS SPORT FOR THE FLY FISHERMAN, EVEN IF HE CAN'T FISH FOR TROUT, AS LONG AS THERE ARE CHUB ABOUT

Generally, well-hackled flies are good for chub; those flies which have a hackle down the body, Soldier Palmer, Red Palmer, Orange Palmer, Orange Bumble, Red Bumble.

The quiet water under trees is not the only place to search for chub with a fly. On many rivers where much wet-fly fishing is done for trout, rivers such as the Teme, the Tees, the Yorkshire rivers and their like, there is often a very big head of chub. And it is usually just where you cease to expect trout that you can begin to expect chub. When a sharp stickly stretch runs down to lose itself finally in slow deeper water, it is where the water loses pace and deepens that the first chub are taken. In such a place there is often a concourse of chub waiting. They like the quiet water with plenty below them, and the faster water brings them much that they can feed on. The wet-fly fisherman can tell at once when it is a chub he has hooked. It is a slower, heavier-feeling fish that tightens his line.

This slowness is characteristic of the chub, and it is important to remember it when your fly is taken. A chub must be given plenty of time to get the fly into its mouth and turn down again. If an interval is not allowed, the fly will be snatched from its mouth by the strike. And if, as is so often the case, the chub is near its holt, under bushes or tree roots, do not let it have its head in the seconds that follow the strike. Get it away quickly or it will surely dive for the roots and smash you.

THE DACE IS A GREAT FLY-TAKER, TOO, BUT YOU NEED TO FISH DIFFERENTLY FROM HOW YOU DO FOR CHUB

FLY FISHING FOR DACE IS A DAINTY BUSINESS. NO BIG FLIES AND SLOW STRIKES AS WITH CHUB

THE SAME 8 OR 9 FT. ROD IS USED, BUT THE 3 YD. CAST IS TAPERED TO 4x OR 5x

ALMOST ANY SMALL FLY WILL DO — BLACK GNAT, OLIVE DUN, RED QUILL, COCH-Y-BONDHU — BUT IT MUST BE SMALL, NOTHING BIGGER THAN N9 OO!

ON MANY RIVERS YOU CAN FISH FROM THE BANK, BUT ON THIS RIVER YOU NEED TO WADE — YOU CAN MANAGE TO COVER QUITE A LOT OF WATER WEARING GUM BOOTS THOUGH THIGH BOOTS ARE BETTER

A BROAD SHALLOW FLAT LIKE THIS IS JUST THE PLACE FOR DACE. BUT YOU MUST WADE QUIETLY TO CATCH ANYTHING. YOU MUST TRY NOT TO MAKE SO MUCH AS A RIPPLE

DEEPER WATER — CHUB

DACE

SHALLOWS

DACE

SHALLOWS

DACE

DACE

SHALLOWS

80

WHERE THE WATER RIPPLES OVER THOSE WEEDS LOOKS A LIKELY PLACE. YOU DON'T NEED TO HAVE MUCH LINE OUT — 7 YDS. FROM ROD TOP TO FLY IS ENOUGH AS YOU'RE BEHIND YOUR FISH

THAT'S IT! — DROP YOUR FLY DELICATELY, RAISE YOUR ROD AS THE FLY FLOATS BACK TO YOU — KEEP IN TOUCH WITH IT SO THAT YOU CAN STRIKE INSTANTLY

81

PICK IT OFF AND CAST AGAIN AS SOON AS IT COMES BACK TO YOU. YOUR FLY CAN ONLY CATCH FISH WHEN IT'S ON THE WATER

PETER WORKS UPSTREAM SLOWLY AND QUIETLY, COVERING ALL THE WATER IN FRONT OF HIM AND CASTING OFTEN

AH, YOU MISSED THAT ONE, PETER — YOU HAVE TO STRIKE LIKE LIGHTNING WITH DACE!

THE DACE TAKES A FLY QUICKER THAN ANY OTHER FISH

Bernard Venables

PRESENTLY ANOTHER DACE RISES, AND AGAIN PETER IS TOO LATE

THAT'S BETTER, PETER — YOU STRUCK AT THE INSTANT IT ROSE

THEN A THIRD ONE RISES TO PETER'S FLY, AND THIS TIME HE HOOKS IT

YOU HAVEN'T DONE TOO BADLY. TO HOOK ONE DACE RISE IN THREE IS QUITE GOOD!

THAT'S RIGHT — WASH YOUR FLY IN THE RIVER AFTER HOOKING A FISH

THEN DRY IT WITH A PIECE OF AMADOU OR YOUR HAND-KERCHIEF AND RE-OIL IT

NOW YOU CAN FISH THIS WATER DOWN AGAIN WITH A WET FLY!

PETER HAS FISHED ALL THE WAY UP THE SHALLOW WATER

THIS IS THE SORT OF FLY YOU NEED FOR IT, A WET FLY WITH "A GOOD ENTRY". IT'S DESIGNED NOT TO OFFER RESISTANCE TO THE WATER. WET IT IN YOUR MOUTH TO MAKE IT SINK

CAST A LONG LINE DOWNSTREAM AND ACROSS AND LET IT WORK ROUND WITH THE CURRENT. STRIKE INSTANTLY AT THE LEAST PLUCK

WHEN THE FLY HAS WORKED ROUND DRAW IN A FEW FEET WITH SHORT DRAWS OF THE LINE WITH YOUR HAND — YOU CAN SHOOT IT WHEN YOU CAST AGAIN. A FISH WILL OFTEN TAKE WHEN YOU'RE DRAWING

PETER CATCHES SEVERAL MORE DACE ON HIS WET FLY

EXCEPT in a water where dace run extra large, it seems rather a waste of their possibilities to fish for them with float tackle.

It must be admitted that the sport they can give fished for thus is fairly limited. They are small fish and can give only little play. And though quick biting they are not very difficult to hook - at least they are not when compared in this respect with large roach. I imagine they are more often fished for with float tackle for live-bait than they are for their own sake.

It is not until they are fished for with fly tackle that they can really be regarded as sporting fish. And then indeed they can give very pretty sport. There is no particular difficulty in inducing them to rise to a fly - they are as free rising as anyone could desire. It is in the hooking of them that the difficulty arises. Their rise is so fast that time after time the fisherman will be caught napping. The strike must really be instantaneous if the fish is to be hooked. An angler who can hook a third of the rises he gets has no reason to be severe with himself. There is just this to be said against fly fishing for dace, that it develops a habit of striking very fast, which is against success when fishing for trout or chub.

Dace are not fussy as to what fly is used. Any small fly will take them. In the mayfly season, however, they have no difficulty in absorbing those monstrous insects.

Dace

The
DACE
and the
GRAYLING

THE dace is rather like a small and more graceful chub. Novices, in fact, often confuse the two species. But this confusion is quite unnecessary. There is one thing alone which can remove all doubt. This is the shape of the anal fin. In the chub it has a convex edge. In the dace it is concave. Besides this, in the chub it is red, and in the dace it is not. The dace may be expected in shallow water of brisk flow.

The grayling is considered by many to be the most beautiful of freshwater fishes. It has that grace of form which only a member of the salmon family can have. And though it has not the bold splendour of colour of the perch and the trout, in its more subtle way it is very beautifully coloured. It is of a general greyish colour, but is suffused with violet, viridian, amethyst, and blue. It is a fine sporting fish for the fisherman all through its season, which is the same as that of the coarse fishes. It is a delicate and difficult quarry for the bait fisherman, and a delight to the fly fisherman. On a river which has grayling, autumn dry fly fishing is a thing not to be missed.

Grayling

The ROACH

the most popular of the fishes

ANYWHERE that coarse fishermen go there will be found the roach fisherman. No other fish has so many followers. From the boys who fish for the little roach of a pond to the experts who pursue their two-pounders, roach fishermen are to be numbered in many thousands. No fish has woven round it more mysteries and expert secrets. A really good roach fisherman is an angler of the most fine and subtle accomplishment.

And he need be, for a large roach is most difficult to deceive, and even that achieved, it is harder still to hook. In still waters or slow, the bite of a roach is often almost imperceptible, and then often so fast that the angler's response must be very quick not to miss it. Once the spell of roach fishing has settled on a man, no other fish can draw him from his love. He is a roach fisherman for life.

NOW FOR **ROACH** ON A FAST RIVER OF THE HAMPSHIRE AVON TYPE — AND YOU'LL SEE HOW A DIFFERENT TYPE OF WATER CAN MAKE AS MUCH DIFFERENCE AS FISHING FOR ANOTHER SPECIES

IN coming to such a river as the Hampshire Avon, the roach fisherman has largely to forget what he has learnt on other and slower waters. To the midland roach fisherman indeed, the tackle used on the Avon is likely at first sight to be horrifying. It will look to him impossibly heavy and certain to scare any roach. But he will be wrong in this. On the Avon he will find lighter tackle would be ineffective. His gossamer gut and sparing shotting would never reach the fish. It would be swept down on the surface, unseen and therefore unheeded by the roach in that clear and heavy current. Many midland and northern anglers do come to the Avon. Some, the fine fishermen that those parts breed, soon adjust themselves. And the adjustment is worth while for the Avon roach is a good fish. But others cannot make the change of outlook that is necessary, and so do not catch the Avon fish. No doubt if they could stay longer they would come in time to understand the river.

NOW, PETER, WE'RE GOING TO FISH FOR ROACH IN THIS FAST CLEAR RIVER. WE MUST FISH FAR OFF BECAUSE THE FISH CAN SEE YOU SO EASILY. AND GETTING YOUR BAIT DOWN TO THE FISH IS MORE IMPORTANT HERE THAN FISHING VERY FINE —

SO WE'RE USING TACKLE THAT WOULD BE IMPOSSIBLY HEAVY ON MANY WATERS A 2X CAST AND A BIG FLOAT TO CARRY A LOT OF SHOT. THE LAST SHOT IS I FT. ABOVE THE HOOK

A LIGHT ROD II FT. LONG WITH SPLIT-CANE TOP IS ABOUT RIGHT. WE'RE GOING TO TRY GENTLES FIRST AS BAIT, SO WE'LL USE A Nº 10 HOOK

70

WEED BED

CHANNEL BETWEEN WEEDS

WEED BED

THERE'S OUR SWIM, BETWEEN THE WEED BEDS — WHERE FISH EXPECT FOOD TO FLOAT DOWN AND WHERE THERE'S ROOM TO SWIM OUR TACKLE

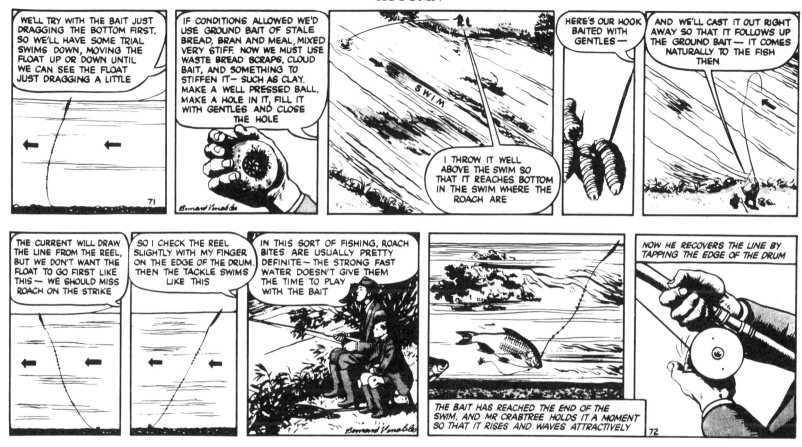

To the newcomer it can be very disconcerting. It is so deep, so fast and yet so glassy clear. The heavy water sweeps down over a thick and brilliant carpet of weed growth. It is those luxuriant weeds that shelter and nurture such fine fish. In the mass that at first may appear unbroken, channels can be detected, clear runs between the weeds over the golden gravel of the bottom. It is in those that the roach can be taken. They live there where the food will come to them, caddis grubs, nymphs, worms washed out of the banks, snails, and many other things. If weirs, piles or other structures are upstream, they will be looking for silkweed too. They are inordinately fond of this, and it is, therefore, a fine bait,

as it is too for many other fish. You need not look long at one of these runs to realise how impossible it is that super fine roach tackle should get down there. Nor would the cloud ground bait of the still water man ever get below the surface. Well weighted tackle and heavy ground bait are essential.

It must not be supposed from this that crude and clumsy tactics are what is required. Fine fishing is relative to the water being fished. The tackle used here is heavy by the standards of many other places, but it is fine for the conditions here. In fact a more elaborately careful approach is needed than is necessary elsewhere. It is useless to sit over these swims and fish under the rod top.

STRIKE! AND A QUICK ONE!

73

THE NEXT SWIM DOWN THE FLOAT DIPS SHARPLY

YOU SEE WHAT FINE BIG ROACH THIS SORT OF RIVER BREEDS, PETER!

AT THE END OF THE NEXT SWIM DOWN, AS MR CRABTREE HOLDS THE FLOAT STILL FOR A MOMENT—

A REALLY BIG ONE THIS TIME. THAT'S OFTEN THE WAY TO GET ONE OF THE GRANDFATHER ROACH!

THE CRABTREES CATCH SEVERAL ROACH THEN BITES STOP

I'LL THROW IN MORE GROUND BAIT

THAT'S SET THEM GOING AGAIN — HERE'S ANOTHER FISH!

74

NO MORE BITES — LET'S TRY A CHANGE OF BAIT

HERE'S A BAIT THAT OFTEN DOES WELL. A SMALL RED WORM. YOU FIND THEM IN HEAPS OF ROTTING LEAVES OR UNDER OLD WET SACKS. I'LL THROW A FEW IN MIXED WITH A LITTLE GROUND BAIT

THE CRABTREES CATCH TWO MORE ROACH ON THE NEW BAIT. THEN SPORT STOPS AND THEY LOOK FOR A NEW SWIM

The water is too clear. Either a swim must be chosen which is well out in the river, and long casts made, or, if the swim is near the bank, it is a case for long trotting. The angler must establish himself well upstream of his swim, and trot his tackle down with the current. The farther off he is, as long as he can see his float well, the more successful he is likely to be.

There is not the same need for him to be close to his float that there is on slower or still water. He will not have to deal with those subtle flickers and barely perceptible movements of the float that are so characteristic of roach in slow water. Here his bites will be far bolder. Usually there will be a sudden decided dip of the float. Then his response must be as quick as it would be anywhere, for not only are the roach quick biting, but with all that length of line out, there is bound to be a certain lag before his strike reaches the fish. This provides another reason for more strength in his line. His strike must obviously be very much harder. The two-pound lines of the quiet water expert would not stand such usage.

The fight of these roach will probably be a revelation to the newcomer from quieter waters. They have a fine muscular tone. In any case playing them at the end of a long line in this strong water has its excitements. Avon roaching is fine sport.

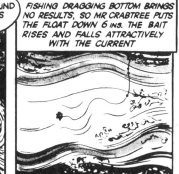

THIS BRINGS SEVERAL GOOD ROACH

MR CRABTREE PLAYS THEM OUT WELL DOWN-STREAM, THEN DRAWS THEM UP ON THE SURFACE, OVER THE TOP OF THE WEEDS

NOW here is the other side of the coin. The Crabtrees are fishing for roach in a canal, and this calls for a style of fishing which has a far wider application than that we have just seen. For every roach taken in the Avon type of water there must be hundreds taken in water that is still or very nearly so. All over the country there are ponds, lakes, canals, and slowly creeping rivers that teem with roach. And in these men fish with styles different indeed from that of the Avon. Whatever variations there may be within these styles there is one common difference from the Avon style. There is here no need to weight the tackle down to the fish in the way there was on the Avon. So you find no heavy weight of lead, no 3x gut. You think in terms of nothing thicker than 6x, and many a midland expert would consider that coarse. Many good roach are taken on gut as fine as 10x and lines that are certainly never above 2 lb. breaking strain.

However, anything quite so cobwebby as this is asking, perhaps, rather a lot of the average fisherman. It takes a very light and practised hand to control a roach of a pound or more on such fine stuff. But he will find that to have any success at all he must make 6x the coarsest gut he will use. Everything must be in proportion: tiny floats, small hooks, and a rod light and very sharp in action. In this rod all the action will be in the tip.

This tip should have an action that is usually called steely, but the truth is that steel does not give the sharp, short and light spring that is essential. There is only one material that is ideal, and that is split cane. Steel is too heavy in feel. The perfect rod for this fishing is made of Spanish reed in the bottom and middle joints, and the top joint of fine stiff split cane. This gives that instantaneous but light response which is needed. It must be light or it would break the fine gut.

You will see that the Crabtrees are not using the cast and hook-to-gut that they usually use. They use instead what is called a one-yard gut bottom. This again is a means of bringing the tackle to its finest. Even that small junction of cast to hook-to-gut is an interruption that is avoided. There is just this one strand of very fine gut below the float. The float itself is often referred to as a toothpick, and that gives an idea of the size it should be. Some fishermen do not use any lead at all on the gut, but merely wrap a little lead wire round the bottom of the float, thus making it self cocking. They like the baited hook to sink with nothing but its own weight. It is an advantage in this style that the bait should sink slowly and gently through the cloud ground bait, appearing to be no more than a part of it. It is the moving bait rather than the still one that brings results.

Gentles are not the only bait that can be used. A very small red worm is good, so is a small pill of paste, or a grain of boiled wheat. The important thing is the ground bait, the cloud bait that drifts down in a hazy mist. A clouding of the water will always attract fish. They will always collect downstream of where horses or cattle wade into the river. Ground bait entices them and excites their appetite but does not feed them. It sets them searching in the murk for the fragments of food that they associate with a clouding of the water. So when they find the angler's bait sinking slowly and waveringly through the cloud, it appears quite

natural to them. Cloud bait can be bought ready prepared in bags, and in present conditions this is an advantage. But the expert dearly likes to prepare his own. He has more faith in it. And when conditions allow, this is how it is done. Put a stale loaf or pieces of stale bread in the oven and leave until dry and crisp. Then grind to a fine powder. At the water side put a small quantity in a clean cloth and wet it so that it can be made into a ball. When it is thrown in, this will enable it to get below the surface, where it will break up and sink slowly in the fine cloud that is required. This style of fishing is called the Sheffield style.

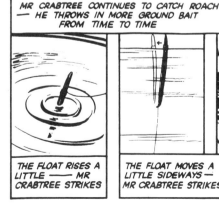

81

The splendid
PERCH

THE perch is a fine, glowing, handsome fish, easily the most handsome of the coarse fish. Many a boy has been set upon the road to becoming a life-long angler by catching a little perch. It would not have been a big perch: just one of those little greedy perch that swarm in many waters and rush at any bait that comes their way. But even so small, it would have had the characteristics of its kind: the splendid colour, the fiercely erected dorsal fin, the general air of find brigandage. The boy would have gazed with fascinated wonderment as he sucked the fingers that had been pricked by the sharp spines of the little fish's dorsal fin, and the angler would have been born in him. Many of us can look back on that, and now, many years afterwards, we can still feel that admiration and excitement at the sight of a perch. For many of us it is a symbol of the lure that makes us fishermen.

Those early perch were easily caught, and those little successes drove us on in the hope of catching the dashing monsters that we knew must be there. But we were soon to find that big perch are not so easily to be taken. A greater skill than ours was necessary, but we went on and gradually the skill came to us. And we found that the bold-taking way of the little perch that so pleased us, was to be found in a perch of any size. At all ages the perch has a bold and satisfying way of taking a bait. It is a way that cannot be mistaken. Those peremptory bobs of the float, those imperious knockings, then the sharp sliding away below the surface. Then the strike and the fight is on. And like everything about the perch, it is a stirring, rushing, tugging business that continues until the net is under him. I still get much of that first thrill when a fine bristling perch is lifted from the water.

YES, PETER, THIS VERY LIGHT SPINNING WITH A THREADLINE OUTFIT IS DELICATE WORK, AND A FINE WAY OF TAKING GOOD PERCH — IT'S THE SORT OF JOB THE REEL IS REALLY SUITABLE FOR!

HERE'S MY THREADLINE REEL. THE SPOOL DOESN'T TURN—THE LINE FLIES OFF LIKE COTTON PULLED OFF THE END OF A COTTON REEL. WITH A SILK OR NYLON LINE OF ABOUT 3lbs. BREAKING STRAIN A LIGHT BAIT CAN BE CAST A LONG WAY. THE SPOOL MUST BE FILLED RIGHT UP TO THE LIP. YOU NEED ABOUT 100 YDS.

PICK-UP FLYER

SLIPPING CLUTCH ADJUSTMENT DIAL

IF A FISH PULLS HARDER THAN THE STRENGTH OF THE LINE, A SLIPPING CLUTCH YIELDS LINE WHETHER YOU'RE TURNING THE HANDLE OR NOT. YOU CAN ADJUST THE TENSION OF THE CLUTCH BY THE DIAL. WHEN YOU START TO WIND IN AFTER A CAST THE FLYER PICKS UP THE LINE AND WINDS IT BACK ON TO THE SPOOL

AND HERE'S THE ROD, 7 FT. LONG SPLIT-CANÉ— COULD BE GREENHEART. IF YOU CAN GET THEM, AGATE RINGS ARE BEST!

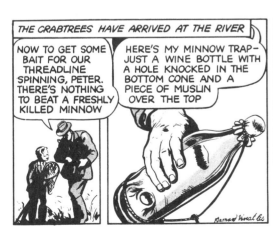

THE CRABTREES HAVE ARRIVED AT THE RIVER

NOW TO GET SOME BAIT FOR OUR THREADLINE SPINNING, PETER. THERE'S NOTHING TO BEAT A FRESHLY KILLED MINNOW

HERE'S MY MINNOW TRAP— JUST A WINE BOTTLE WITH A HOLE KNOCKED IN THE BOTTOM CONE AND A PIECE OF MUSLIN OVER THE TOP

WE PUT IT IN THE SHALLOW WATER WHERE THE MINNOWS CONGREGATE WITH THE BOTTOM FACING DOWNSTREAM AND A PIECE OF BREAD INSIDE FOR BAIT. SEE, PETER, THEY'RE GOING IN!

MR CRABTREE PULLS UP THE TRAP AND PUTS THE MINNOWS IN A BOTTLE HALF FULL OF WATER. THE SHAKING OF THE BOTTLE IN HIS BAG WILL AERATE THE WATER AND KEEP THE MINNOWS ALIVE. BUT HE KILLS ONE BY A FINGER FLICK ON THE HEAD TO MOUNT ON A SPINNING FLIGHT

SEE, PETER, I PUSH THE LEADED PIN INTO THE BAIT— PUSH THE SPIKE OF THE UPPER HOOK INTO ITS SIDE AND THEN BIND WITH SOFT WIRE

AND HERE'S THE TRACE — 3 x GUT OR NYLON. 2 FT. LONG WITH A TINY SWIVEL AT THE TOP AND A LOOP ABOUT 4" LONG AT THE BOTTOM

15

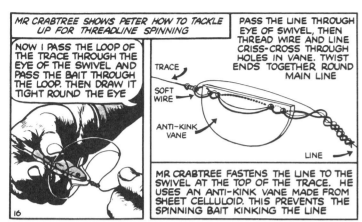

NOW Peter is being introduced to a method that has its own specialised uses and as such is good sport. But it is unfortunate that it is greatly abused. The fault of the threadline reel is that it is capable of too many uses. And for many of these it is a substitute for skill. It is too easy. Anyone can learn to cast with this reel in half an hour, and then he has in his hands a weapon that can be devastatingly effective. He can catch fish with ease that would not otherwise have been his until he had acquired a proper skill with far greater practice. And why not, you may say. Why shouldn't we enjoy this success as soon as possible? Because a large part of the enjoyment of angling is the pitting of skill against the instincts of the fish. Merely to catch fish with ease, divorced from all else, cannot satisfy a real angler for long. There is no triumph in it. Who can congratulate himself on a success that has not been earned? The beginner, yes. At first it is sufficient for him to catch a fish. That is triumph enough without worrying much about how it was caught. But if a man is a fisherman at all, this phase passes. If it did not it would be simpler for him to use a net or dynamite. He is no fisherman.

Skill is not the only thing that grows with experience. So also does a sense of responsibility towards the water and the interests of anglers generally. A man comes to realise that fish stock must be conserved. He sees that unbridled slaughter will soon denude a water of fish, and then no one will have fishing. A beginner cannot be expected to realise this as an older angler does. If he can he will carry away with delight his bag of corpses. The threadline reel puts in his hands the means of doing this. It is like putting a gun in the hands of a boy before he realises its dangers. No angler should touch the threadline reel until he has served an apprenticeship with more skill-demanding tools. Let him learn to float fish with a flick'em reel or an aerial. They are perfect for the method. Let him learn to cast his tackle with those. And let him learn to play a fish with no slipping clutch to act as a buffer between him and losing his fish. He should learn to make his skill a buffer.

Let him learn to spin with a centre pin reel or a multiplier. Let him learn so to control his gear that he does not have overruns. Only when he has learnt these things is he fit to use a threadline reel. Then he can be trusted with it. He will not use it for anything but its proper purpose. And when he catches large numbers of fish with it he will not kill them. He will have learnt restraint. He will not, in fact, have the desire to kill his fish.

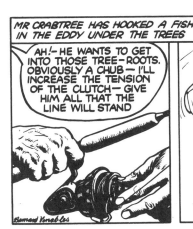

He will already have had that which makes fishing worth while for him. In trout fishing it is legitimate to take a certain number of fish for the table. A carefully managed trout stream or lake can generally stand a modest bag of kept fish for the fisherman. But it is seldom that this can be said of coarse fish waters.

Threadline enthusiasts will often tell you that in fact the reel does require a great deal of skill. To flick a bait, they say, into all sorts of small places demands much skill, and only the threadline reel can do it. This is largely an illusion. The reel is a fine thing for patting you on the back. It gives you a sense of skill which would quickly evaporate if you tried a more ambitious method.

A fly fisherman can put his fly in those places too, but he needs very much more skill to do so. A good float fisherman can send his tackle where he wants it, but his skill is a real and solid thing, not an illusion.

I remember fishing with a man on a trout stream that was much fished. He spun with a threadline reel, I fished dry fly. He caught six trout, I caught a brace. But subsequently when he tried the fly, though he was a fly fisherman, he could not get one trout, though I could still get my brace.

And now having condemned the threadline reel so thoroughly for purposes for which it is not designed, what is its

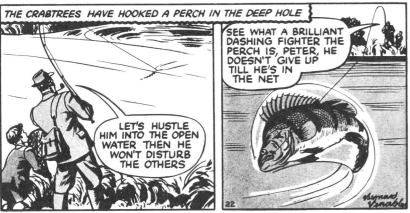

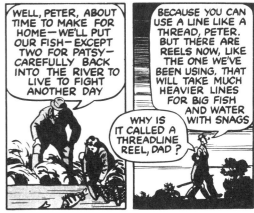

proper use? It was designed in the first place for conditions of very low clear water and bright sunshine. Under these conditions, which often occur in July or August, fly fishing becomes impossible. At first it is still possible to get trout with a dry fly rather than a wet one, but soon fly ceases to be of use at all. Then the only thing that will catch trout is a minnow, and that must be spun upstream. A reel is needed that will cast a very light bait and spin it in as little as six inches of water. It was for this purpose the threadline reel was designed. With it the angler can work slowly upstream casting ahead of him into every likely place, and spinning the bait back to him at the pace of the stream or rather faster.

Having a left-hand wind no time is lost by changing hands. When fishing in very shallow water, the fisherman can start to wind before the bait touches water. So that when it does actually enter the water the bait is already spinning. There is no other reel that will perform just this job. It can cast baits for the very smallest weights and cast them long distances, though a great deal of the time long casting is unnecessary in this upstream fishing for trout.

From this original purpose to certain forms of coarse fishing is quite a short step. As the Crabtrees show here, it is a good way of spinning for chub and perch, and as such can show some good sport.

TO TACKLE RUDD YOU NEED TO GO AFLOAT, PETER — BUT DO IT QUIETLY. IT'S NO GOOD ROWING RIGHT UP TO THE FISH!

FISHING for rudd is, like the fish themselves, superficially like fishing for roach. But to get the best out of the fishing, they must be treated in a specialised way. Not perhaps in the case of river rudd. Treat them like roach and you are likely to do as well thus as any other way. But it is mostly in lakes that you will fish for rudd, and it is here that you must treat them as a special case. Plenty of rudd are caught while fishing for roach in the usual way, but this is not the way to get good bags of them.

It is worth while going for them specially, for where they are they are usually present in very large numbers. And if only you can avoid alarming them, you can have very good sport indeed. It is not only that they are free biters and plentiful, but also that they are weightier fish than roach and, therefore, can give a better fight. A bright sunny day is good for rudd.

The Crabtrees show one method of fishing which will yield many fish, but it is not the only way.

continued on page 92

NOW, PETER, THERE ARE PLENTY OF RUDD IN THIS LAKE, BUT WE DON'T WANT TO GO NEARER TO THEM THAN WE CAN CAST WITH THE WIND BEHIND US. AND WE **MUST** GO QUIETLY!

BY THE REEDS IS THE PLACE TO FIND THEM — I THROW IN A SLICE OF BREAD THAT HAS BEEN BAKED HARD AND ANCHOR IT WITH A PIECE OF STRING AND A STONE. I'LL DO THE SAME IN SEVERAL OTHER PLACES

NOW SEE HOW THE RUDD HAVE COME ROUND TO NIBBLE THE BREAD

WE'LL USE A SMALL FLOAT AND MAKE IT SELF-COCKING BY WINDING LEAD WIRE ROUND THE BOTTOM OF IT

NOW THE ONLY WEIGHT BELOW THE FLOAT IS THE SMALL RED WORM WE USE AS BAIT ON THE Nº 10 ROUND-BEND HOOK

The RUDD *the golden fish of the lake*

SUPERFICIALLY the rudd is like the roach, but the fisherman should very soon come to see the difference between them. The obvious and definite difference is that in the rudd the dorsal fin is set much farther back than in the roach. Also the lower lip of the rudd projects while that of the roach recedes. But there are other differences which though not so definite soon become equally obvious. The rudd is altogether a more colourful, handsome fish. It is suffused all over with a shine of gold. Its eye is more red than the eye of the roach. And all its fins are red, while the roach's are not. Only its ventral and anal fins are so. But beyond this the rudd is a bulkier fish,

a fine thick-shouldered solid fish. It is indeed very handsome.

It is primarily a lake fish, and it is as such that the angler usually fishes for it. As a river fish it is less sought and less easy to find. It is only found in the slower rivers.

Its most famous home is the Norfolk Broads, and there it is in Heigham Sound that it most particularly thrives. Another famous rudd fishery is Slapton Leigh in Devonshire. It is a very common fish in Ireland, where, in the manner of most fish, it grows to much greater weights than it does here. It is known there as the roach. There are no true roach native to Ireland.

It is the practice in Norfolk to bait-up in advance bays in the reeds. Then at the time of fishing the boat is moored well upwind of the swim - twenty to twenty five yards, so that the wind helps casting. Then the tackle, often quite heavy, is cast into the swim. Casting from the coil is the usual way, but the Avon cast, shown elsewhere in this book, should do equally well. If the fish are going to take at all, they will usually do so quickly, and you may be into your first fish almost at once. And mind it does not plunge straight into the reeds and smash you. The first rush of a good rudd may take some holding.

Another and more mobile way, and one which requires no ground bait, is to watch the edge of the reeds. If the rudd are feeding you will see a few of the reeds sway, independently of the others or of any wind. This means that rudd are feeding by them, taking insects, snails and so forth that cling to them. Cast your tackle up to where you see the movement, and you may have a good fish. Then transfer your attention to the next place along the reeds where you see this movement. Moving on all the time you can sometimes collect a good bag. Evening is a good time for it. You must, of course, stand well off from the reeds. If you bring your boat too close in you will certainly alarm the fish.

Another and very enjoyable way to take rudd is by fly fishing, more particularly dry fly fishing. Rudd are very good fly takers, and will accept almost any fly you like to offer them.

Here again, evening is a good time. Sometimes on a warm evening rudd may be seen rising all over a lake. Again along the reeds is a likely place, and if you can get someone to row you very quietly along them but some way out, you can cast in to the rises you see. If you see no rise, cast your fly close to the reeds and let it rest there for a minute. Giving a twitch is sometimes effective. This makes it skate across the surface, always a good technique for rudd. A sedge fly pattern is good for this.

If you are alone in the boat you can often do a drift down the lake, casting on all sides of you as you go. A very light air, just enough to give you a slow drift, is what is needed. Too fast a drift will set your fly dragging too quickly. Often a lake will have just the faintest current through it towards its outflow. This can be used on those still windless evenings in fine weather which so often set all the rudd taking flies.

Mr. Crabtree shows you how a combination of the fly rod and bait fishing can also be used. But even here the fly will often do as well as bait. When the rudd begin to worry your slice of bread, cast your dry fly up to them. They will often take it well.

If a preference for certain flies must be given, these would probably do as well as any: Black Gnat, Coch-y-bondhu, and some sedges.

PETER CASTS OUT AGAIN

WHEN HE LETS HIS BAIT HANG STILL IT IS IGNORED

BUT THE SLOWLY SINKING BAIT BRINGS RESULTS —

BUT ONLY FOR A TIME

THEY'VE STOPPED FEEDING, PETER. THE FREQUENT CASTING OF THE FLOAT PUTS THEM OFF AFTER A TIME. LET'S MOVE ON TO ONE OF THE OTHER PIECES OF BREAD WE PUT IN

I'LL TRY HERE, PETER— WITH A FLY ROD, A 3 YD. TAPERED CAST, AND ONE OR TWO GENTLES ON A Nº 12 HOOK-TO-GUT

MR CRABTREE'S BAIT DROPS LIGHTLY AMONG THE FEEDING RUDD

HE IS SOON PLAYING A FISH WHICH FIGHTS WELL ON THE LIGHT TACKLE

HE CONTINUES TO CATCH THEM WITHOUT DISTURBING THE OTHERS

YOU SEE, PETER, THERE'S NOTHING TO DROP WITH A SPLASH AND ALARM THEM AS THERE IS WITH A FLOAT TACKLE !

THE WEATHER'S MILD, PETER, WE MIGHT TRY SOME PERCHING — IT'S NOT MUCH GOOD GOING FOR PERCH IN HARD WEATHER!

PERCH fishing is stirring sport. It is a joy to the boy beginning to fish, and equally one to the oldest veteran. It does not require such acute concentration as some forms of fishing and is therefore, in a sense, more restful. You can give yourself up to the fun of it. And exciting fun it can be. There is no temporising about a perch that takes a bait. It takes boldly and unmistakably. It gives you plenty of warning, and pulls the float well under. And when it is hooked it fights with every ounce of itself, finally coming to the net glowing and defiant. You might say that you get your full money's worth from a perch.

And another advantage about perch fishing is its mobility and freedom. You are not tied to a spot and you carry no ground bait. You can wander down the river looking for perchy spots, and this in itself is keenly enjoyable. It is when you come to the deepest, most mysterious corners, the most unplumbed-looking holes,

THE CRABTREES ARE BY THE RIVER AGAIN, TO FISH FOR PERCH — Bernard Venables

WELL, THERE'S THE TACKLE READY, PETER — ROD 12 FT. LONG-UNDRESSED SILK LINE OF ABOUT 6 lbs. BREAKING STRAIN, WELL GREASED TO MAKE IT FLOAT — 1 YD. OF 3 X GUT CAST — A No. 6 HOOK TO GUT — A FLOAT AND, OF COURSE, A REEL

WE PINCH SPLIT SHOT ON THE CAST TO TAKE THE BAIT DOWN TO THE FISH — COCK THE FLOAT WITH JUST THE TOP SHOWING ABOVE THE SURFACE

THERE ARE MANY REELS OF THIS TYPE, PETER, THEY'RE VERY FREE RUNNING AND SENSITIVE TO FINGER CONTROL ON THE SMOOTH EDGE OF THE DRUM-LIKE THIS. THE CHECK IS CONTROLLED EITHER BY A LEVER LIKE THIS OR BY A BUTTON ON THE BACK OF THE REEL

NOW HERE'S A TYPICAL PERCH HOLE. THEY LOVE DEEP QUIET PLACES OUT OF THE WAY OF THE CURRENT AND AGAINST CAMP-SHEATHING OR AMONG OLD PILES — YOU ALWAYS FIND PERCH IN SHOALS

WE'D BETTER FIND THE DEPTH FIRST WITH THE PLUMMET

LOOK, I PASS THE HOOK THROUGH THE RING AT THE TOP AND STICK IT LIGHTLY INTO THE CORK AT THE BOTTOM — THEN LOWER IT QUIETLY INTO THE WATER. THIS TELLS ME THE DEPTH, THEN I'LL SET THE FLOAT SO THAT THE HOOK IS ABOUT 2" OFF THE BOTTOM. WE HAVE TO GET DOWN TO THE FISH AT THIS TIME OF THE YEAR

BENEATH THE SURFACE OF THE EDDY—

that you think, here will be perch. It is in those dark murks of water that are so fascinating in themselves that you find the perch. And you find them in those holes against bridge piers, and stage piles, and bank shedding: oddly attractive places that are enticing anyway. Then out of these dark, deep, shadowed waters, you draw this flashing, splendid fish. In this, somehow, is the whole essence of fishing. Here somewhere is the very kernel of that which so grips the imagination of the fisherman.

But, of course, the perch is not a fish of the rivers alone. It is equally a lake fish. Though it is a keen pleasure to catch perch anywhere, I think it is particularly in a river that it is so fascinating.

In a lake you are to some extent deprived of the fun of seeking those perchy places, and this is a real loss. Two rivers that come specially to my mind in this connection are the Wye of Hereford, and the Kennet. On both I have had good perch fishing, but more particularly the Wye. This is a really fine perch river. I remember a stretch where it did not seem there was a perch under a pound. Time after time they would turn up at all weights from a pound-and-a-half upwards. Occasionally a three-pounder would be taken. Such fishing is apt to be a thing of the past now. It need not be. Beat pollution and conserve stock, and there may be much fishing like this.

In conclusion . . .

IT is right that this book should be concluded with certain general facts useful to the fisherman. And the first of these is one that will not be fresh to the reader, but cannot be emphasized too much. That is the absolute necessity of being quiet. There are so many ways in which the angler can forget himself in this respect, and yet be unaware of it. A heavy footfall, knocking a pipe out on the gunwale of a boat - such little things as this can be disastrous.

Equally important is the need to keep out of sight. This does not necessarily mean that the angler must not stand up. It is more than anything a matter of background. If the fisherman is a shape against the sky or a light background, he is obvious to the fish. But if there is a background behind him of trees or rocks or some such thing, he will melt into it even if he is standing - unless of course he is wearing a white shirt without a coat. He should avoid having the sun behind him so that his shadow falls on the water, and if he fishes at night, the moon is equally likely to keep the fish from him.

In the handling of all hook baits and ground baits, he must have clean hands. The least taint of, for instance, tobacco is fatal.

Tackle should be looked after to preserve it and to make it function well. Wet lines should be stripped from the reel and dried on a line drier or the back of a chair. Gut should be stored in the dark or it will rot. Flies should be protected against moths. Reels should be kept well oiled or they may jam unexpectedly. In any case their life is prolonged. When out of use fly lines should be taken off the reel and hung in loose coils in an airy place. Without this they are liable to go sticky, and for this there is no real cure.

If swivels are to work properly they should be oiled. The last few feet of all lines should be well tested from time to time. If they have become weak, break off line until you come to a part that is still strong.

In many places, before you may fish, it is necessary to buy a licence. Enquiry should always be made about this. Licences can generally be bought from certain hotels or inns near the fishing, from fishery board offices, from water bailiffs or some other accredited person. This licence is in addition to any ticket that may have to be bought for private fishing.

A final fundamental rule of fishing is never to behave in a way that will interfere with the sport of others, and to pay strict regard to the rights of farmers and other holders of the land beside the water. Shut all gates, do not tread down crops, do not leave any litter, or take any risk of causing fire.

Printed by WPG Ltd, Welshpool, Powys SY21 7DF